Medical Law in Argentina

AF703826

Medical Law in Argentina

Juan Bautista Torres Lopéz

This book was originally published as a monograph in the International Encyclopaedia of Laws/Medical Law.

Founding Editor: Roger Blanpain
General Editor: Frank Hendrickx
Volume Editor: Herman Nys; Associate Editor: Tom Goffin

Wolters Kluwer

Published by:
Kluwer Law International B.V.
PO Box 316
2400 AH Alphen aan den Rijn
The Netherlands
E-mail: lrs-sales@wolterskluwer.com
Website: www.wolterskluwer.com/en/solutions/kluwerlawinternational

Sold and distributed by:
Wolters Kluwer Legal & Regulatory U.S.
920 Links Avenue
Landisville, PA 17538
United States of America
E-mail: customer.service@wolterskluwer.com

DISCLAIMER: The material in this volume is in the nature of general comment only. It is not offered as advice on any particular matter and should not be taken as such. The editor and the contributing authors expressly disclaim all liability to any person with regard to anything done or omitted to be done, and with respect to the consequences of anything done or omitted to be done wholly or partly in reliance upon the whole or any part of the contents of this volume. No reader should act or refrain from acting on the basis of any matter contained in this volume without first obtaining professional advice regarding the particular facts and circumstances at issue. Any and all opinions expressed herein are those of the particular author and are not necessarily those of the editor or publisher of this volume.

ISBN 978-94-035-2837-3

e-Book: ISBN 978-94-035-2847-2
web-PDF: ISBN 978-94-035-2857-1

This title is available on www.kluwerlawonline.com

© 2023 Kluwer Law International BV, The Netherlands

All rights reserved. No part of this publication may be reproduced, stored in a retrieval system, or transmitted in any form or by any means, electronic, mechanical, photocopying, recording, or otherwise, without the prior written permission of the publisher.

Permission to use this content must be obtained from the copyright owner. More information can be found at: www.wolterskluwer.com/en/solutions/legal-regulatory/permissions-reprints-and-licensing

The Author

Juan Bautista Torres López (h) was born in 1988 in Buenos Aires, Argentina. He is a lawyer graduated from the Universidad de Buenos Aires (UBA). He is also a journalist graduated from 'Taller Escuela Agencia (TEA)' School of Journalism. He is a partner at TORRES LOPEZ ABOGADOS, responsible for the practice area of Health Law that specializes in litigation against social security, health insurance and 'pre-paid medicine' companies on issues of: affiliation, disability, assisted reproduction techniques and medication, supplies and therapies supply. He is author of numerous articles on specialized doctrine as well as a regular media consultant on medical and healthcare legal matters. He has been a legal and public policy consultant at the National Argentine Congress for political parties, and advisor at the Council of the Judiciary of the City of Buenos Aires. Currently, he is the Coordinator of the Argumentation, Legal Writing and Clear Language magazine of the URBE ET IUS publicatio, and Deputy General Director of the General Directorate of Legal Affairs of the Obra Social de la Ciudad de Buenos Aires (ObSBA). He is considered an expert and 'media influencer' on Medical Law, with thousands of followers on social networks such as Instagram and YouTube.

The Author

Table of Contents

Table of Contents

List of Abbreviations

AIDS	Acquired Immune Deficiency Syndrome
ANMAT	National Administration of Drugs, Foods and Medical Services
ANSSAL	Administración Nacional del Seguro de Salud or National Healthcare Administration
AMA	Argentine Medical Association
AMBA	*Área Metropolitana de Buenos Aires*, or Metropolitan Area of Buenos Aires
ARS	Argentina Peso
CABA	Cuban American Bar Association
CAEME	Cámara Argentina de Especialidades Medicinales
CBC	Ciclo Básico Común
CELS	Social and Legal Studies Centre
CPCNN	Civil and Commercial Procedural Code of the Nation
CNACAF	National Federal Administrative Court of Appeals
CNCiv	National Civil Court
COFESA	Confederation of Employers in South Africa
CONEAU	National Commission for University Evaluations and Accreditations
COMRA	Medical Confederation of Argentina
FORA	Argentine Obstetrics Association
HIV	Human Immunodeficiency Virus
HPGD	Decentralized – Management Public Hospital Regime
HPV	Human Papillomavirus
IAR	Rotating Annual Internship
INCUCIA	National Central Institute – Unique Ablation and Implant Coordinator
INDEC	*Instituto Nacional de Estadística y Censos or* National Institute of Statistics and Census
IVE	Voluntary Interruption of Pregnancy

List of Abbreviations

INSSJP or PAMI	National Institute of Social Services for Pensioners
LGBT	Lesbians, Gays, Bisexuals, and Transgender
OFHERHUS	Federal Observatory of Human Resources in Health
PGD	Preimplantation Genetic Diagnosis
PHO	Panamerican Health Organizaton
PNGCAM	National Program of Quality Assurance of Medical Assistance
PMI	Maternal Infantile Plan
PMO	Obligatory Medical Program
QS	Quacquarelli Symonds
REFEPS	Federal Network of Healthcare Professionals Registries
SANO	Automatic Nominative Subsidy
SAME	System of Medical Assistance in the Emergency Room
SISA	Integrated System of Argentinean Sanitary Information
SUR	Unique Reimbursement System
SSSalud	Superintendence of Health Services
TRA	Assisted reproduction techniques
UBA	Universidad of Buenos Aires
UCA	Universidad Católica Argentina
UNCUYO	National University of Cuyo
UNLAM	National University of La Matanza
UNLP	National University of La Plata
UM	Morón University
USA	United States of America
US	United states
USD	United States Dollar
WHO	World Health Organization
WMO	World Meteorological Organization

Preface

The present work is the result of a risky and curious series of challenges that exceed personal vertigo. In the first place, it is a volume dedicated to Health Law in Argentina, thought, written and presented in the height of a world pandemic. I do not know how many times it will be possible to write and narrate about the health system in midst of a health crisis that crossed all possible frontiers and that – naturally – came to change ideas and conceptions in the midst of the writing of the work. The task then implied explaining a technical framework while that same framework was mutating or being put in check, a framework which, it must be said, in Argentina is still gaining strength: the reader will find in the first pages of this work that Argentine Health Law is still a developing subject, nourished by the criteria of Justice and somewhat chaotic due to its fragmentation in the rules.

But beyond these challenges – writing about Health in the midst of a world pandemic, in a country that is still shaping its Health Law – it also implied a personal challenge. In this, I must thank Wolters Kluwer, the publishing house that, in addition to giving me the opportunity to carry out this work, has been patient and has provided me with invaluable support in the process. In the same way, I am grateful for the advice and trust placed in me by Professor Pablo Ferrara, who, besides being a brilliant colleague –whose scrolls would not fit on this page – is a dear friend. I also owe gratitude to my friends, who without knowing (or pretending to know) about the health system and the incidence of law in this field, listened to my long conversations about the encyclopaedia. To my family, for their support and encouragement. And to Patricia, my wife, whose support, love and serenity were a master key for me to sit down and continue when everything – the text, the confinement, the pressure of deadlines and the obsessive commitment with which I embrace a project of this magnitude – was uphill.

Finally, I would like to mention two colleagues and partners of TORRES LOPEZ ABOGADOS: my father Juan Bautista and my brother Isaias, whose blind trust in each of my initiatives is for me a balm and a guarantee. To my father –an inexhaustible source of inspiration – I also owe my passion for Law, an unrepeatable and necessary engine to complete this work, which also comes to bring a part of me closer. Like Health Law in Argentina, we are still in process. The good thing is that we are the ones who write history.

General Introduction

§1. General Background of the Country

I. Geography

1. Argentina is located in the southeast of the American continent and is bordered to the north by the Plurinational State of Bolivia and the Republic of Paraguay, to the south by Chile and the South Atlantic Ocean, to the east by Brazil's Federative Republic, the Republic of Uruguay's Oriental Republic, and to the west by Chile. It is the fourth-largest country in America and the eighth-largest country in the globe:[1] Its total surface area is 3,761,274 km2, of which 2,791,810 km2 are on the South American continent and 969,464 km2 are on Antarctica (South Georgia and South Sandwich). The maximum width reaches 1,408 km, whereas the maximum width from north to south is 3,694 km. Only in the area of continental America, Argentina's territory spans 15,000 km. The territorial sea, which extends up to twelve nautical miles inland, is the area of the sea over which Argentina exercises exclusive sovereignty. It has ice fields, mountains, plateaus, plains, dry regions, forests, rain forests and lakes all over its territory, making it one of the most biodiverse nations in the world. The highest peak in the nation is Mount Aconcagua, located in the Mendoza province (6,960.8 m. above the seal level). The Great Depression of San Julián, a basin located 105 m. below sea level, is in the province of Santa Cruz, on the other hand, and is the location of the lowest point.[2]

1. If we were to consider the territories claimed, Argentina would be 7th among the countries with the largest surface.
2. https://www.ign.gob.ar/NuestrasActividades/Geografia/DatosArgentina/MaximasAlturas.

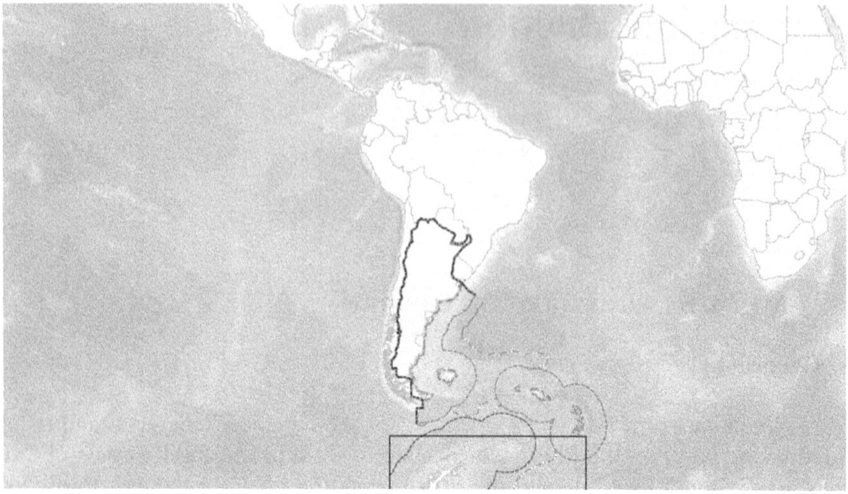

II. Cultural Composition

2. Argentina is frequently referred to as a 'melting pot,' which is due to the fact that thousands of immigrants have come to settle there over the course of its history, resulting in a forced cultural composition that recognizes Argentina as one of the most significant receiving countries of the transatlantic migration by the end of the nineteenth century and in the early twentieth century.[3] In 1914, three out of ten residents were born abroad. Since then, European immigration – mainly from Italy, Spain, Poland and the former Yugoslavia – to Argentina has decreased, while the number of people from border countries or other regions of the United States (US) has been steadily increasing, mainly from Bolivia, Peru and Paraguay.[4]

3. The ethnic and cultural picture of Argentina is completed by its aboriginal communities or indigenous peoples, which represent about 3% to 5% of the total population, although no conclusive data or official information is available from the national census.[5]

III. Political System

4. Argentina has federal, republican and representative forms of government, according to Article 1 of the Argentine National Constitution, which are the cornerstones of the country's legal system. Likewise, this same legal structure provides for

3. http://www.mininterior.gov.ar/poblacion/pdf/Diagnostico_de_las_poblaciones_de_inmigrantes_en_Argentina.pdf.
4. http://www.mininterior.gov.ar/poblacion/pdf/Diagnostico_de_las_poblaciones_de_inmigrantes_en_Argentina.pdf.
5. https://www.cels.org.ar/common/documentos/informe_2002_cap_11.pdf.

the federal government to support the Roman Apostolic Catholic Church (section 2 – NC). Representation means a government run by representatives of the people; Republican means these representatives are elected by popular vote. The Constitution, adopted in 1853 and subsequently amended in 1860, 1898, 1957 and 1994, is the supreme statute. In turn, power is divided into three branches: executive, legislative and judicial. These three branches check each other, leading to decentralization and balance. Finally, federation means that the provinces have their own autonomy even though they are united by the national government.

5. As for the representative form, as Roberto Gargarella says, 'the concept of representation refers above all to the sovereignty of the people, which is the original source of power and is in turn linked to a set of procedures and principles that arise from the stages fundamental'[6] of Argentine constitutionalism.

6. The government system in Argentina is presidential and democratic. Voting is universal and compulsory from the age of 18. Act 26774 extends the right to vote in state elections to persons between the ages of 16 and 18 who are not considered offenders if they do not vote.

IV. Population and Vital Statistics

7. Based on data from the National Geographic Institute and information and projections collected during the 2010 Population, Household and Housing Census (INDEC in Spanish), in 2020 Argentina reached a population of 45,376 763 inhabitants, with a continuous increase over the last decade (in 2010 it was 40,117,096 inhabitants, in 2015 it was 43,131,966).[7] Nearly 32% of the total population lives in the Metropolitan Area of Buenos Aires – better known as (AMBA) in Spanish, a name which includes the Autonomous City of Buenos Aires and Greater Buenos Aires – the most populous metropolitan area. Greater Cordoba (3.6%), Greater Rosario (3.1%) and Greater Mendoza (2.3%) represent some of the major urban areas in the country. Data collected from the 2010 census showed that 36,517,332 people lived in urban areas while 3,599,764 lived in rural areas. The Autonomous City of Buenos Aires, unlike other jurisdictions, has no rural areas.

8. According to the World Health Organization's 2020 reports – Monitoring Health for the SDGs (Sustainable Development Goals) – life expectancy in Argentina is estimated at an average of 76.9 years (73.5 years for men; 80.3 years for women): nearly five years longer than the world average life expectancy. Healthy life expectancy is 68.4 years (65.9 for men; 70.7 for women).[8]

6. https://aulavirtual4.unl.edu.ar/pluginfile.php/7032/mod_folder/content/0/Gargarella%20Roberto%20-%20Republicana%20representativa%20y%20federal%20-%20pag%203%20a%2023.pdf?forcedownload=1.
7. https://www.ign.gob.ar/NuestrasActividades/Geografia/DatosArgentina/Poblacion2.
8. https://apps.who.int/iris/bitstream/handle/10665/332070/9789240005105-eng.pdf.

V. Social and Cultural Values

9. The multiple religions, origins and beliefs that coexist in the Argentine territory have contributed to the development of an eclectic culture, difficult to define due to its richness and complexity. The National Survey on Religious Beliefs and Attitudes in Argentina,[9] conducted in 2019 by the Society, Culture and Religion program of the Centre for Research and Studies at Work (dependent on CEIL-CONICET, the main institution engaged in the promotion of science and technology in Argentina), reveals the values that characterize the very heterogeneous population live in this country.

10. This survey indicates that the Catholic religion is losing members in the country, even if it still has the majority (62.9%), while non-believers (18.9%) and evangelicals (15.3%) are on the rise. The fact that the last pope, Francesco, whose real name is Jorge Mario Bergoglio, Argentine, did not motivate people to change their religious life.

11. Regarding abortion, this CEIL-CONICET survey finds that between 2008 and 2019, the proportion of those who consider abortion to be a woman's right has doubled (in 2019, 27.3% of those questioned support the freedom to abort, provided that the pregnant woman makes this choice). Finally, it should be mentioned that in December 2020, the National Congress passed a law establishing the voluntary termination of pregnancy. Likewise, it is claimed that most Argentines question concepts of patriarchal family and the roles of men and women in the home, which in this sense shows an evolving critical society.

12. Although Argentina's criminal law does not provide for the death penalty, half the population is in favour of this type of punishment for serious crimes. Conversely, 7 out of 10 respondents are in favour of stricter migration controls. In terms of education, 94.3% agree that the public university must still be free for all and are against social plans: 59.3% believe that this laxity is fuelling.

§2. General Description of the Healthcare System

I. General Review of the Healthcare System

A. Introduction

13. The Argentine healthcare system has undergone numerous changes and additions over time. As for the health system as we know it today – with its foundations of solidarity and justice – it is worth noting that major changes took place in the late 1980s. Since the beginning of the twenty-first century, this process has accelerated with the emergence of new specific rules establishing rights and obligations for the beneficiaries of the system that cover a fragmented regulatory map, not

9. http://www.ceil-conicet.gov.ar/wp-content/uploads/2019/11/ii25-2encuestacreencias.pdf.

always equally intertwined and in some respects overcrowded with laws, decrees, administrative decisions, ordinances and jurisprudence that do not correspond to each other.

14. This health system is made up of three main sectors: the public sector (the state), the private sector (the prepaid pharmaceutical companies) and social security (the health insurance plan managed by the Union). Furthermore, there are three levels within the public sector: national, provincial and municipal. This system has not always been like this and although there are no common criteria for identifying the different stages in the history of the Argentine healthcare system, it can be classified as follows:[10] (1) until 1945; (2) from 1945 to 1955 – centralized planning; (3) from 1955 to 1970 – pluralist model of decentralized planning; (4) from 1970 to 1990 – consolidation and crisis of the fragmented system; (5) from 1990 to 2001 – deregulation of the health markets; and (6) from 2001 up to date. In practice, some events marked the changes in the system, such as the first and second presidency of Juan Domingo Perón (from 1946 to 1952 and from 1952 to 1955); the emergence and development of the Union-managed health insurance plan in all sectors; the progressive withdrawal of the state and the subsequent advancement of prepaid health insurance; the development of regulations to better address the health sector.

15. After the outbreak of the COVID-19 pandemic, a new historical era has begun, the beginning of a seventh phase still to be written: not in terms of a paradigm shift, but in terms of the necessary adaptation of the system, in view of cooperation. International between states and even the private sector in the race to research, test, manufacture and distribute vaccines before the virus worsens the international situation.

B. *Short Progress Regarding Changes in the System*

16. When Juan Domingo Perón assumed office in June 1946, it signalled the start of this democratic government and the end of a de facto one. This implied the emergence of a new Welfare state model, a concept that called for the formulation of rules and regulations aimed at enhancing the workers' quality of life generally. The State's involvement in healthcare up until 1945 was subsidized, condensed, isolated, and more concerned with immediate issues than with preventative measures. At the time, there was no concept of the right to health as it is now, which is more focused on achieving the highest quality of life (not strictly related to illnesses). The province's first Ministry of Health and Labour was established during those times,

10. This distinction, literally quoted in the article by Matías Salvador Ballesteros entitled 'El sistema sanitario argentino: un análisis a partir de la evolución de los establecimientos de salud desde mediados del siglo XX a la actualidad' ('The Argentinean Sanitary System: an analysis on the evolution of the health institutions as from the mid-20th century up to date') (National University of Cuyo, School of Political and Social Sciences – Publications Centre; Millcayac- Digital Magazine of Social Sciences; 4; 6; 3-2017; 147-174; available at https://ri.conicet.gov.ar/bitstream/handle/11336/77618/CONICET_Digital_Nro.24e06d38-1e6e-4b3c-bdf6-38547bf7fb2d_A.pdf?sequence=2&isAllowed=y) is precise, educational and concrete.

specifically in 1941 in the province of Santa Fe,[11] a necessary antecedent of a change in paradigm that was bound to take place. A powerful statement made by Perón in 1944 before a group of doctors as the vice-president of the de facto government prior to his election as president is as follows: 'The public health is designed to extend the life of an average human being for 10 to 20 years. Gentlemen, if this wasn't enough, we wouldn't need a ministry of public health. There shouldn't be any spending restrictions on public health. The country's need to treat its sick citizens must set the limit'.

17. Beginning in 1946, when the Public Health Secretariat was officially established as a ministry and under the leadership of Dr Ramón Carrillo, who oversaw the National Ministry of Health, is when this new conception first emerged. Public health is now on the national agenda for the first time. The growth of the union movement and a number of initiatives, such as paid holidays for employees, the By-Laws of the Rural Worker, and the expansion of the social security system, also helped to frame the significance of health on a large scale. Perón would even change the National Constitution, which would help him win re-election and dedicate the rights of workers and the elderly and children.[12]

18. The aforementioned signs indicated a shift into the beginning of a new model that would ripen until the present and that would be distinguished by universalizing access to health, even though the idea of charity was still more deeply ingrained than solidarity. The transition from a liberal system, where health plays a subsidised role and is not a people's right, being State limited to not impede the natural pace of the market and being the donations the principal support of sanitary actions, to a State more engaged with the population's access to the health system, can be used to summarize this change.[13] This process hasn't been simple or linear, and it's experienced both successes and failures along the way.

19. In terms of public health, the State started to take a more proactive and accountable role as of 1945. In addition to the system's growth, the union sector expanded its influence and created the Union-run Medical Insurance Plan. The number of beds per subsector was a sign of this change: in Argentina, public hospitals had 63,000 beds in 1946, but by 1958, this number had risen to 97,319 beds, accounting for 80% of the total.[14] The remaining 20% was made up of 15% by the private sector and 5% by the union-run Medical Insurance Plan (6,028). (17,903).

---

11. https://iris.paho.org/bitstream/handle/10665.2/3477/argentina-salud-publica-historia-tomo2.pdf?sequence=1&isAllowed=y.
12. El libro de los presidentes argentinos del siglo XX (The book of the Argentinean Presidents of the 20th Century) 2000, Ed. Aguilar, Buenos Aires, Argentina.
13. https://salud.gob.ar/dels/entradas/el-modelo-de-salud-argentino-historia-caracteristicas-fallas.
14. Federico Tobar makes a more generous estimation and affirms that 'between 1946 and 1951 4,229 sanitary institutions were built, 35 of which were big policlinics all over the country. This represented the duplication of the public hospital beds from 76,300 in 1946 to 134,218 in 1954. This meant 7.4 beds every 1000 inhabitants, which was twice as much as the case nowadays (3.9 beds every 1,000 inhabitants)' ('Breve historia del sistema argentino de salud', (Brief history of the Argentinean Health System) by Federico Tobar, 2012 available at https://www.mendoza.gov.ar/salud/wp-content/uploads/sites/16/2017/03/Modulo-2-Tobar-historia-SSA.pdf).

By 1969, this figure had changed: although the total number of beds had increased by subsector (to 133,847), the private sector had made the largest contribution, bringing the total up to 30,095, or 22% of the total. The public sector at that time held the remaining 74% of the beds, while the union-run Medical Insurance Plan only occupied 4% of them. There was yet another phenomenon in 1970: the distribution of institutional and regulatory responsibilities among the provinces, which would gradually relieve the federal government of its obligations and pave the way for the implementation of the first Peronist administration's policies.

20. The derogated Law 18610, which was passed in 1970, gave registered workers access to the Union-run Medical Insurance Plan and gave employers the obligation to make the required contributions in each industry. The National Institute of Social Services for Pensioners was established the following year by Law 19032, bringing these users under the umbrella of the program. Consequently, the Union-run Medical Insurance Plan at the start of the 1980s provided coverage for close to 70% of the populace. Since the Union-run Medical Insurance Plans served as the system's financial institutions, this expansion was not reflected in charts comparing the capacity of the Union-run Medical Insurance Plan's institutions or beds to those of the State or the private sector. Instead of using all of their available resources, they agreed and hired from the private sector. However, they also created harsh tension between the public sector and the social security system, both of which were supported by the State, which resolved the system's and the resources' fragmentation.

21. In this context, the private sector thus finds a very attractive way to access healthcare in Argentina: the idea of health as a commodity crystallized in the last decade of the twentieth century. The growth of the private subsector, strongly driven by government policy itself, with prepaid pharmaceutical companies leading the way, is reflected in several indices. In 1969, the private subsector made up 38% of public health institutions. In the year 1995, this number represented 55%. To the detriment of this, and compared to the same years, the public sector fell from 58% to 44%. In 1969, there were a total of 6,469 establishments; in 1995, there were 16,066 (for reasons already explained) to complete as interest and private sector increased in Argentina contracted state involvement in relation to health. The public option was limited to those who did not have a union-run health insurance plan or private insurance. In short, aid in public hospitals has been reduced to people with the lowest incomes.

22. By the 1990s, the Argentinean economic context – and specially the financial crisis – seriously affected the integrity of the Union-run Medical Insurance Plans. Polices tending to reduce the cost of the waged workers implied a decrease in the contributions supporting social security. At that time, the regulatory scheme that is currently framing the Medical Law started to take shape: The law of the Union-run Medical Insurance Plan, (1988), the Decree 9/93 allowing the beneficiaries of social security to freely choose in certain contexts (1993), the Medical Obligatory Program (PMO by its acronym in Spanish-1996, Resolution 247/96) and the Obligatory Medical Program (PMO) of Emergencies (2002), with its amendment in the year 2004; the system of Social Security Disability Benefits (1997), the law of Pre-paid Medicine Companies (2011), among other fundamental norms for the current scheme.

23. In the twenty-first century, several specific rules about certain pathologies began to proliferate in Argentina such as those of eating disorders; rare illnesses; Diabetes; Law of Transplants; Law of medicinal use of cannabis and its derivatives; mental health; among others to ensure the obligation to assist patients with special health conditions. This type of standard, while constituting the basis of coverage for the beneficiaries, also highlights the lack of the system on the part of the actors of the subsectors, i.e., those who are called upon to provide the service and to provide certain benefits are among those who receive more complaints from users.[15] The framework is completed by the Superintendency of Health Services – an entity created by the 1996 decree, responsible for the regulation and control of the actors of the national health insurance system and whose main purpose is the control of doctors managed by the 'Union of Insurance and Prepaid Pharmaceutical Companies – without the tools to comply with the law and impose exemplary penalties on providers who violate standards, in many cases in the usual way. The systematic violation of users' rights is inevitably settled in court, most often by way of health amparos or summary proceedings.

II. Regulation of the Healthcare System

A. *General Regulatory Frame*

24. Considering that the Argentine healthcare system consists of three subsectors: public, private and social security, the regulatory framework of each subsector can be analysed separately; however, union health insurance schemes, pre-paid insurance schemes and even national systems may often have common legal frameworks for health aspects.

1. National Constitution

25. Regarding the general legal framework, the highest is the National Constitution of Argentina. While the Carta Manga in no way expresses the value of all citizens' constitutional rights to health and optimal quality of life, the existence of guidelines and frameworks of reference, ideally, is especially true.

15. According to the report drafted by Ombudsman's People Office of the Province of Buenos Aires, of the 59,617 claims received in the year 2019, 33% corresponded to complaints related to the health system. Only claims for public services (35%) exceeded that number. After that, there were those for road matters (15%), social security (10%) and consumption (8%). Of the total of claims due to health issues, 36% belonged to claims for medicines, 21% for medicine practices, and 13% for prosthesis, among others. The report can be consulted at https://www.defensorba.org.ar/contenido/los-servicios-publicos-lideraron-el-ranking-de-reclamos-en-la-defensoria.

26. Section 42 of the National Constitution provides that: 'Consumers and users of goods and services have the right in relation to consumption, to the protection of their health, safety and economic interests; to accurate and truthful information, to freedom of choice, and conditions of equitable and humane treatment. The authorities shall provide for the protection of said rights, the education for consumption, the defence of competition against all forms of markets distortion, the control of the natural and legal monopolies, the control of quality and efficiency of the public utilities, and the creation of consumers and users' partnerships. Legislation shall establish efficient procedures to prevent and solve disputes, and the regulatory frameworks of the national public utilities granting the necessary participation of consumers and users' partnerships and of the interested provinces, in the control entities'. Even though the definition of 'consumer' – Ley 24240 – has brought about controversy in the field of Medical Law, the case law is clear in terms of protecting the users of prepaid medicine and this has been extended to those belonging to union-run medical insurance plans and health services in general.[16]

27. Another reference worth mentioning of the Argentinean Fundamental Law is found in section 75, subsection 22 which enumerates among the National Congress' powers that of 'passing or dismissing treaties celebrated with other nations and with international organizations and the concordats with the Holy Seat. The treaties and concordats take precedence over the laws'. In summary, this section gives constitutional status to the international instruments signed by the country, introduced by the 1994 constitutional amendments, which address a series of efforts that Argentina clearly commits to achieving basic health standards.

28. This is the case of Article XI of the American Declaration of the Rights and Duties of man, under which it is established that 'Every person has the right to the preservation of his health through sanitary and social measures relating to food, clothing, housing and medical care, to the extent permitted by public and community resources'; or Article 25 of the Universal Declaration of Human Rights which sets forth that 'Everyone has the right to a standard of living adequate for the health and well-being of himself and of his family, including food, clothing, housing and medical care and necessary social services' and that 'Motherhood and childhood are

16. The National Federal Civil and Criminal Court, one of the branches with the most matured and solid criteria in Argentina regarding health, has repeatedly ascertained the obligations of the public sector, the pre-paid medicine companies, and the union-run medical insurance plans. A case in point: Room I strictly observed that 'the Health Insurance providers -companies of pre-paid medicine, union-run medical insurance plans and by extension' other providers – such as the Buenos Aires University Bureau of union-run medical insurance plan, sued in the case cited, an agency with 'constitutional autonomy, from the Buenos Aires University, as a legal, self-sufficient and autonomous person under public law (s. 75, subs. 19 of the National Constitution)' – 'are bound to accurately inform its members in relation to the scope of the benefits of their plan (s. 4 under the Consumer Protection Act). Beyond that, the answer given by the Health Insurance Provider must contain the facts and the rules supporting their position, for the interested party to exercise his right to be informed (s. 4 of the cited law) and to receive the assistance for type of problem the beneficiary has and with the corresponding humane treatment (s. 8 of the cited law).' (Case: 'M., V. against DOSUBA about Amparo of health', CCF 7387/2017/CA1, decision of the Room I of the Federal Civil and Commercial Court dated on 20/11/2020).

entitled to special care and assistance'; or the American Convention on Human Rights – Pact of San José of Costa Rica – even more clearer the additional Protocol to that Convention – known as Protocol of San Salvador – in which under Article 10 provides the scope of the 'Right to health', 'understood to mean the enjoyment of the highest level of physical, mental and social well-being', recognizing health 'as a public good'.

29. Subsection 22 of section 75 of the National Constitution gives a more extensive list of international instruments with a higher status than that of the laws: the International Covenant on Economic, Social and Cultural Rights; the Covenant on Civil and Political Rights and its Optional Protocol; the Convention on the Prevention and Punishment on the Crime of Genocide; the International Convention on the Elimination of all Forms of Racial Discrimination; the Convention on the Elimination of all Forms of Discrimination against Women; the Convention against Torture and other Cruel, Inhuman or Degrading Treatments or Punishments; and the Convention on the Children's Rights which establishes that 'under the conditions of their validity, they have constitutional rank, do not abolish sections of the first part of this Constitution and must be considered as complementary to the right and guarantees herein set forth. They shall only be reported by, in its case, the National Executive Power with the prior approval of two-thirds of the total members of both Houses'. The same section imposes new obligations on Argentina, as it confirms that 'all further covenants and conventions on human rights, after being passed by the Congress, shall require the vote of the two-thirds of the total members of each House to enjoy constitutional rank.'

2. Obligatory Medical Program

30. The National Constitution, as well as the international instruments included at the top of the legal pyramid, helped define the nature of Argentine medical law. The PMO is one of the main legal cornerstones in today's Medical Law architecture. The PMO is the set of basic benefits guaranteed by the Health Insurances Providers, companies of pre-paid medicine[17] and the State. The local case law has best defined the PMO, affirming in countless occasions that it was conceived as a minimum regime of benefits that the subsectors are to guarantee; 'such Program does not constitute a limitation for the healthcare providers, but rather a non-restricted enumeration of minimum benefits that beneficiaries are entitled to demand' from

17. The PMO does not mention the pre-paid medicine companies due to a chronological matter: the law regulating these companies- 26682- was created in the year 2011. Such regulation, however, establishes under its s. 7, the obligation from the part of these companies 'to cover, at least, in their medical assistance plans the Obligatory Medical Program in force according to the Resolution of the National Ministry of Health and the System of Basic Benefits for Disabled People set forth in the law 24901 and its amendments.'

prepaid and union – run medical insurance entities, 'and it contains a set of obligatory services – a base of benefits below which no individual is supposed to be placed in no context whatsoever'.[18]

31. Resolutions 201/2002 and 310/2004 of the Ministry of Health contain the substance of the PMO and in its whereas, there are the pillars supporting the structure created by the Program. So as to contextualize and get to understand the reasons why a country conceives the need for basic and universal coverage for all its inhabitants, it is necessary to consider that Argentina has lived in a sanitary emergency since 2002 without intermission, when the National Administration passed the Decree 486/2002 which declared the National Sanitary Emergency due to the 'highly critical' financial and economic situation, which made 'institutionally obligatory to introduce the necessary and suitable mechanisms to face the exceptional difficult situation' in a very 'serious context' characterized by 'current intolerable poverty levels; a crisis affecting the health, a deep production stagnation with the consequent fiscal disorder and its complement political crisis which affects the provincial states as members of the national organization', the way the Decree 486/2002 put it.

32. The above citations are in accordance with the terms of the statute. It is worth mentioning that the brutality and drama of the decree are far from exaggerated, but it contains the dark side of Argentina's history: the so-called Crisis of 2001, an event that affected the country all over the world. In January 2002, Law No. 25561 and under Article 76 of the National Constitution, which declares 'a state of emergency in society in the social, economic, administrative, financial and external situation', which also helps to characterize the difficult times and chaos in the country those days.

33. Resolution 201/2002 is created in this context with a country under general emergency after the resignation of a president before the end of his administration. Therefore, the PMO establishes that 'the essential and basic benefits shall be deemed those necessary and irreplaceable for life conservation and assistance to illnesses which the National Health System and the National Institute of Social Services for Pensioners shall guarantee for the time of the emergency. Hence, the National System of Health Insurance shall tend to guarantee equity, universality and solidarity for all the beneficiaries'.

34. This triad – equity, universality and solidarity – are part of the backbone of the Argentinean Health System the way we know it today. The PMO further considers other issues: '... prevention illnesses polices are to be prioritized over the curative actions based on the different sociodemographic characteristics in every National Healthcare System Provider's community'; 'in a Sanitary Emergency, everyone must be guaranteed access to the health system, and especially the most

18. Case 'Barzana, Macarena Soledad against IOMA about Amparo', National Federal Civil and Commercial Court Room I; 29/04/2010; Secretary of case law of the National Federal Civil and Commercial Court; 5927/2004; RC J 4588/14.

vulnerable such as pregnant women, school-age children, people over 65 and those covered by special laws' among other main principles of the PMO. Somehow, not only does the PMO constitute a key ruling piece, but it is also a declaration of principles in terms of sanitation, a Manifesto, and a plan of action with non-negotiable notes.

35. PMO has access to basic services such as our primary healthcare (including the infant fertility program), women's cancer prevention program, and specialty care such as cardiovascular, geriatrics, ophthalmology, pediatrics, and nutrition, among others. The PMO also determines the coverage percentages to be paid by union-run health insurance and prepaid plans for drugs, service specifications (Annex II), drug lists, pharmacological groups and nutritional formulas (Annex III) and drug reference price lists (Annex IV) and other specifications.

3. Special Laws

36. The essence of Argentina's health system can be drawn from the country's constitution and the PMO. These guidelines and the already mentioned pillars – justice, universality, solidarity, prevention before treatment, priority for the most vulnerable – are the basis for compiling a set of medical legal norms (some of which even predate the WMO). Medical law has flourished over the past three decades with all kinds of regulations, from laws to decrees and ministerial resolutions. The large number of instruments, which effectively translate into clause-based legislative models for specific claims or cases, merits criticism as to whether a single body or at least a stricter scrutiny of existing norms is needed. So, does it have sense to pass special laws for every single pathology (as is the case now) or it is better to have concrete control legislation?

37. Inside this normative set, it is worth mentioning some of the main instruments, namely:

– Law 22431: on the integral protection System for the disabled.[19] It establishes 'a System of integral protection for disabled people, tending to guarantee medical assistance, education and social security, as well as to give them franchises and stimulus allowing them to neutralize their disadvantage the best way possible and

19. The fact the law speaks about 'the disabled' and 'people with a disability' deserves a comment which is not minor in the twenty-first century. The referred law was passed in the year 1981: on the one hand, after four decades, we can affirm that we are now conscious about the fact that a disability does not define a person and that first and foremost it is his/her quality as a human being; therefore, talking about 'disabled' is neither right nor accurate. On the other hand, it should be noted that the law had been signed by a de facto president: an example of militaries that got rid of democracy, took the government by force, and committed the most atrocious crimes for which some of them were tried and condemned, and were indifferent to even notice if their ways were either right or inclusive.

to give them opportunity, making their best effort, to perform a role in their communities equivalent to the one played by normal people'.[20] (section 1). In turn, this law deems people with a disability as 'all individuals having a functional permanent or prolonged physical or mental condition that in relation to their age and social condition would imply considerable disadvantages for their family, social, educational and labour integration' (section 2).

- Law 24901: on the System of basic benefits of integral assistance and rehabilitation for people with a disability. It establishes 'a system of basic benefits of integral assistance for the people with disabilities, guaranteeing prevention, assistance, promotion and protection actions, so as to grant an integral coverage of their needs and requirements' (section 1). This set of benefits is obligatory for all the subsectors of the Health System. This law considers 'an individual with a disability' – and not 'a disabled person' the way the 22431 used to do it – as 'an individual who suffers a permanent or prolonged functional, motor, sensorial or mental alteration that according to his age or social context indicates considerable disadvantages for his familiar, social, educational or labour integration' (section 9).

38. Among the basic benefits (Chapter IV of the law) there are preventive benefits (section 14), rehabilitation benefits (section 15), educational therapeutic benefits (section 16), educational benefits (section 17), social security benefits (section 18) and 'specific services', drafted 'for the sole purpose of being descriptive' and the ones 'integrating the basic benefits to be given to the person with a disability in accordance with the criteria of the pathology (type and grade), age, socio-familiar situation, being it possible to be modified or enlarged by the norms' (section 19). Among the latter, there are early stimulation (section 20), initial education (section 21), basic general education (section 22), labour training (section 23), day-care centre (section 24), educational therapeutic centre (section 25), psycho–physical rehabilitation centre (Article 26), motor rehabilitation (section 27) including rehabilitation and assistance treatments of orthosis, prosthesis, technical help and other orthopaedic devices, and 'integral dental assistance, which can cover from the primary to the complex surgical and rehabilitation techniques', and in if necessary, the coverage of an anaesthetist (section 28) are included. The last line is essential because PMOs offer limited dental coverage compared to the other specialties listed here.

39. The law for disabilities also provides 'Alternative systems different from the family' (Chapter VI) in case 'the person with a disability cannot stay with his/her family of origin'; 'at his own or his legal representative's request, he shall be entitled to be introduced into one of the alternative systems apart from the family, namely: residences, small homes and homes' (section 29). The criteria to determine the characteristics of those resources shall be age, type and grade of disability, level

20. The same as the previous footnote, the fact that the norm makes a distinction between 'normal people' and people with a disability, assuming that a person with a disability is not a 'normal' person, speaks about an anachronical register about disability (and about an apparent normality). Under the current reality, that implies a discriminatory and even ignorant act due to its inaccuracy.

of self-dependency and independency. Last but not least, this plexus establishes the obligation to cover 'complementary benefits' (Chapter VII), such as economic coverage (section 33), labour introduction (section 36), psychiatric assistance (section 37), total coverage of 'medicines or specific diet therapeutic products and those not produced in the country' (section 38) total coverage of diagnosis and control studies, and of those 'specialists not belonging to the body of professionals which would be necessary to participate due to the specific characteristics of the pathology' according to certain parameters (section 39):

- Law 23753: on diabetes. This regulatory plexus is about 'diabetes and its complications'. Article 5 defines one of the most important points related to coverage, that is, '100% (100%) medication coverage for diabetes patients and reactive medication for self-monitoring diagnostics according to the dose prescribed by doctors'. In order to gain access, 'a medical certificate about the patient's condition must be obtained from the state institution. Such a certificate must be issued at the time of diagnosis and is valid as long as the patient's condition is chronic. The Authority of the Application shall not extend the requirements of authorization to have access to the coverage'. The same section establishes that the Authority of Application shall have the obligation 'to perform national disease awareness and detection campaigns, for the society to be well-informed about this pathology and the patients to be socially integrated the best way possible' and 'to articulate educational programs allowing students as well as teachers in all the levels in the local jurisdictions to have the necessary knowledge about this condition'.
- Law 26396: on eating disorders. It declares the prevention and control of eating disorders of national interest, clearly affirming that it will cover the research of the causing agents, the diagnosis and treatment of the diseases related thereto, the integral assistance, and rehabilitation, including that of derived pathologies, and all measures tending to prevent its dissemination. The rule describes an eating disorder as obesity, bulimia, and nervous anorexia, 'and any further disease that the regulations establish that is in relation with inadequate eating habits'. This last phrase widens up the universe of eating disorders and even makes eventual analogue interpretations in relation to 'inadequate eating habits'.[21] The law created the National Program of Prevention and Control of eating disorders to implement informative campaigns, promote healthy nutritional behaviours and meet other social demands.
- Law 27350: on the medicinal use of cannabis and its derivatives. It establishes the regulatory framework for the medical and scientific research of the medicinal, therapeutic and/or palliative use of cannabis and its derivatives for pain guaranteeing and promoting integral healthcare. At the same time, it creates the

21. Even though in some legislation it is impossible to have a legislative technique so 'permissive', this is very frequent in the Argentinean Health Law, maybe because the lawmakers are well aware of the technological breakthroughs – which obviously also affect the field of medicine, which are well ahead of the regulatory incorporations and even due to the gap in between one another (even more considering that more often than not developments in treatments and medicines are first approved in the USA and Europe and once they are tested – almost converted into scientific truths known worldwide – are incorporated to the local legislation).

National Program for the Research and Study on the Medicinal Use of Cannabis plant, its derivatives, and non-conventional treatments, within the Ministry of Health whose aim ranges from 'actions to promote and prevent the right to health' to 'efforts to know about the side effects of the medicinal use of cannabis and its derivatives, and ways to establish security and limitations for its use to guarantee the population's well-fare'. Because this is a new law – passed in November 2020 – there is a long way to go in terms of its observance greatly influencing not only the patients but also areas of law such as the criminal one.[22]
- Law 25673: it creates the National Program of Sexual Health and Responsible Procreation. Apart from the creation of the program and its objectives, section 6 of the law establishes the suitable health control system for the early detection of sexual transmission diseases; the prescription and supply of contraception methods and elements which have to be reversible, non-abortive[23] and transitory, respecting the receiver's criteria and convictions – unless the physician specifically indicates otherwise – and previously gives the information about advantages and disadvantages on the natural methods and those approved by National Administration of Drugs, Foods and Medical Services (ANMAT); and the regular controls after the use of the method chosen. To establish the obligatory base desired, the aforementioned benefits must be included in the PMO, in the national medical practices' nomenclature and the pharmacological nomenclature. Moreover, the public system health services and those of the social security and the private systems must incorporate them into their coverages on an equal basis with other systems (section 7).
- Law 27491: on the Vaccine-preventable diseases. As a premonition, this law was passed at the end of 2018. Only a year later, the world was going to be shaken by a terrible pandemic: this norm constitutes an eloquent framework about the significance and value that Argentina has given to vaccination, 'a preventive public health strategy', considered as a social good, and subject to five basic principles established under section 2 of this instrument: 'a) Cost-free vaccines and access to vaccination services with social equity for all stages in life; b) Obligation for all inhabitants to be vaccinated; c) Prevalence of public health over personal interest; d) Availability of vaccines and vaccination services; e) Participation of all health sectors and others related to their social determinants, with the aim of reaching satisfactory vaccination coverages in a sustainable way.'

40. As it can be noted, Law 27491 similarly replicates the principles sustaining the Argentinean Health Law already been depicted. This regulation also declares vaccination of national interest, 'this being understood as the research, the epidemiological surveillance, the decision-making process based on the evidence, the acquisition, storage, distribution and provision of vaccines, ensuring the cold chain as well as the production and all the measures tending to foster vaccination in the population and to strengthen vaccines safety surveillance' (section 3); as well as the

22. Drug possession is criminalized in Argentina.
23. The wilful interruption of pregnancy bill – abortion- in Argentina, at the end 2020, forces to reinterpret this statement, or else, to read it in context.

approval of the National Vaccination Calendar established by the authority of application and the provision of vaccines contained in such schedule together with 'those recommended by the sanitary authority for risk groups and those indicated in an epidemiological emergency situation, which are compulsory for all the inhabitants of the country pursuant to the guidelines set forth by the authority of application' (section 7). Failure to observance of this obligation and others of the same plexus shall entitle the corresponding sanitary authority to take measures tending to make the vaccination effective, ranging from the notification to the compulsive vaccination (section 14). Hence, in certain circumstances and for certain segments of the population, vaccination is imperative and the failure to compliance may even entail legal consequences:[24]

– Law 26529: on the patient's rights regarding their relationship with the health institutions and professionals. Not only does this law establish the essential rights a patient enjoys in relation to the health professionals, insurance providers or effectors, but it also contains concrete guidelines about sanitary information, informed consent, or clinical history. Thus, it provides an organizational scheme and concrete definitions about these concepts and their scopes.

41. The patient's right is the right to help – without discrimination or prejudice based on the patient's ideology, religious or political beliefs, socioeconomic status, race, gender, sexual orientation or other circumstances, as the surrogate professional may be exempted from providing assistance. such patients in the presence of another competent specialist, who is actually the responsibility of the patient – the right of the patient and his family or companions to dignity and humanity, the right to intimate relationships, the right to confidentiality, the right to accept or refuse a certain treatment or medical or biological procedure without giving reasons, and withdraw your notices of intent in the future; to receive the necessary sanitary information about one's health and even the right not to receive such information; last but not least It is not important to get written health information to get a second opinion on the diagnosis, prognosis or treatment of their medical condition:

– Law 23798: It declares that the fight against Human Immunodeficiency Virus (HIV) is in the national interest and defines this fight as the discovery and research of its causative agent, diagnosis and treatment of the disease, prevention, assistance and rehabilitation, including its derived pathology, and measures aimed at prevention. its spread, The first is the education of the population. In

24. Among recent background case law, we can consider the decision issued in the case entitled 'D., S. R. against B., A. F. about family incident', from the National Civil Court of Appeals Room D, dated on 28/09/2020. There, the judges confirmed a ruling of original jurisdiction that compelled, ordered and summoned the parents of a girl, within the term of 48 hours, to go to the medical institution and/or vaccination centre belonging to their medical coverage or to a public hospital to have the girl vaccinated with the triple bacterial vaccine, Human Papillomavirus (HPV) and the rest of the National Vaccination Calendar of Argentina, under penalty of performing the vaccination in a compulsive way with the intervention of the Medical Emergency Assistance System (SAME in Spanish) and the Police of the Autonomous City of Buenos Aires and of applying a progressive and exemplary fine.

addition, according to it, the requesting authority is responsible for: (a) the development of a plan designed to fulfil the activities mentioned in the first part of this paragraph, manage resources for its financing and implementation; (b) Promote the human resources' training and foster research activities development, coordinating them with other national, provincial or municipal sectors and international public and private agencies; (c) Apply methods ensuring high quality and security; (d) Comply with the information system to be established; (e) Promote the celebration of international agreements to formulate and develop programs related to the objectives of this law. Finally, he explains that it is the Executive that takes measures to inform the population about the characteristics of Acquired Immune Deficiency Syndrome (AIDS), its causes or possible routes of transmission and spread, the recommended preventive measures and the appropriate treatments for its cure, in order to avoid unscrupulous biased dissemination. (Section 4 of the law).

- Ley 26689: on Rare Diseases. A disease is rare when the number of people affected is equal or less than one per two thousand (1 per 2000), in relation to a national epidemiological situation. It introduces an extensive and ambitious list of objectives among which the following are to be highlighted: to promote the access to healthcare of the people with rare diseases, including actions aiming at the early detection, diagnosis, treatment and recovery in the frame of the effective access to the right to health for all the people; to promote, in its context, and together with the sanitary jurisdictional authorities, the creation of an multidisciplinary institution specialized in rare diseases, which can implement policies, strategies and actions for the integral care of the people with rare diseases and their families; to foster the development of regional centres and services of reference specialized in the assistance of people with rare diseases, with the suitable technology and professionals and the adequate allocation of funding; to stimulate the development and production of medicinal products for the early detection, diagnosis, treatment and recovery of the people with rare diseases, among others.

42. The same as the other regulations regarding health, this law specially mentions the subjects bound to comply with it. Clearly stated are 'the union-run health insurance plans framed in the laws 23660 and 23661, the health insurance of the National Judicial Power, the Social Assistance Bureau for the National Congress' Staff, the pre-paid medicine entities and the entities providing services to the universities staff as well as those providers rendering medical services to its members regardless of the judicial status they possess', as well as those having the responsibility to 'give medical assistance to people with rare diseases, including as a minimum the benefits determined by the authority of application'. At the beginning of the year 2021, the list of rare diseases was over 5,800 which explains the wide scope of the norm when talking about the 'integral health care' of the people with these conditions:

- Law 26657: on Mental Health which derogated Law 22914. This law changes of paradigm about mental healthcare and ensures 'the full enjoyment of human rights by those with a mental impairment living in the national territory, recognized in international human rights instruments with constitutional hierarchy, notwithstanding more beneficial regulations for the protection of these rights established by the provinces and the autonomous city of Buenos Aires'. As a distinctive note, addictions are contemplated 'as part of the policies of mental health' (section 4), the right of individuals with mental impairment is set forth (section 7) and the health assistance 'in the hand of an interdisciplinary team of professionals, technicians and other skilled workers with the suitable license issued by the competent authority', including the areas of psychology, psychiatry, social work, nursing, occupational therapy and other pertinent disciplines and fields are provided to that respect. (Section 8).

43. Section 14 provides one of the main innovations of this norm, when considering the admittance at a hospital as a therapeutic resource of restrictive character: '... it can only be used when it gives greater therapeutic benefits than those interventions in the family, community or social context. The communication of the patient with the family, friends, social and labour contacts should be promoted, unless otherwise established with well-grounded reasons with well-grounded reasons by the intervening health team', section 14 reads. At the same time, hospitalization should be as short as possible according to interdisciplinary standards of treatment, and in no case should hospitalization be prescribed or prolonged due to social or housing problems. Therefore, the state is obliged to provide the necessary resources for this purpose through competent state institutions. (Section 15).

44. One of the most controversial points of this rule is in section 27, which briefly establishes the progressive definite closure of mental hospitals in Argentina. Hence, the creation of new mental monovalent-admission asylums, neuropsychiatric hospitals or institutions is prohibited whether they are public or private; and in the case of the existing ones, they should adjust to the principles and objectives exposed until they are replaced by alternative institutions. This adaptation or replacement can mean neither the reduction of the personnel nor the decrease of the right acquired thereof. This is a controverted objective as the regulation in this section established that the definitive replacement of the mental institutions and asylums *supra* referred should be met in the year 2020 at the latest, pursuant to the Panama Council, adopted by Regional Conference of Mental Health convened by the Panamerican Health Organizaton (PHO) – World Health Organization (WHS) '20 years after the Declaration of Caracas' in the City of Panama on the 8th of October 2010. The truth is that the deadlines are over, it is not happening, the law is in arrears with compliance and uncertainty in its application, staffing agencies and even private sector agencies say they cannot adapt to the guidelines of the new regulations.[25]

25. This is the case of the Social and Legal Studies Centre (CELS in Spanish), which has emphatically denounced the failure to compliance of the regulations from the part of other institutions.

B. Special Regulatory Framework

45. When we consider the set of rules that make up the healthcare law and the basic benefits that all individuals, regardless of their insurance type, must receive, we find that both union-run insurance and prepaid drug companies are regulated under special rules. So the state is consolidated not only by subsidized providers – those without prepayment or union insurance – but also by a general regulation that, while broad, does not provide for a specific legal framework that would determine the rights of prepaid pharmaceutical companies. The liability of a specific organization, such as an insurance plan administered by a union.

1. Union-run Health Insurance Plans

46. Laws 23660 and 23661 are the basis of the rights and duties framing the health insurances and their beneficiaries in Argentina. To those two laws, we must add other regulations such as Decree 446/2000 – which guarantees every member the right to choose a different union-run health insurance plan which complies with specific characteristics, once a year – or Decree 1305/2000, which adopted certain sections of Decree 446, among other legislative texts.

47. Law 23660, under section 1 enumerates the subjects affected by this regulation – union-run health insurances plans, those of state-owned companies, those incorporated by an agreement with state-owned or private companies, those of the civil and military security forces' staff and any other entity created or to be created to perform the activities established under this law, setting clear that the union-run health insurance plans shall allocate their resources primarily to health benefits, apart from giving other social benefits (section 3). Moreover, it clearly set forth the entities' funding, the resources' allocation, and the universe of beneficiaries they shall focus on. (sections 8 and 9).

48. Said section 8 reads:

Those entitled to be beneficiaries of the health insurance hereinunder.

(a) The workers under a contract of employment, whether that is in the public or private sector of the Executive Power or in its autocratic and decentralized agencies; in state-owned companies or partnership, in the municipality of the city of Buenos Aires and in the National Territory of Tierra del Fuego, Antártida and the South Atlantic Ocean islands; (Subsection replaced by Section 2 of Law 23890 B.O. 30/10/1990)
(b) National pensioners and retirees and those of the Municipality of the City of Buenos Aires
(c) *Beneficiaries of national non-contributory benefits.*

Section 9 widens the scope of users when including as beneficiaries those as follows:

(a) Primary family groups of the categories indicated in the previous section. Primary family groups are deemed to be those integrated by the beneficiary´s spouse, single children until they are twenty one, non-emancipated due to the age or professional, commercial or labour activity, the single children of over twenty one years of age until they twenty-five inclusive,[26] who are exclusively under the guardianship of the beneficiary and are studying regular courses recognized by the competent authority, the disabled children and under the guardianship of the beneficiary, over twenty one; the spouse's children; the underaged whose physical custody has been established by judicial or administrative authority meeting the requirements under this subsection;

(b) The person living with the beneficiary that has the same ostensible family treatment, under the regulation set forth in the norm.[27]

The National Health Insurances Bureau shall authorize – according to its own requirements- the inclusion of other blood ascendants or descendants under the beneficiary's custody in which case an additional contribution of 1.5% is fixed for each family member included.

49. The Health Insurance Law further provides some solutions of continuity for the beneficiary in case the main beneficiary is dismissed, dies, is suspended or is on an extended unpaid leave of absence, among other events (section 10) and gives details about the formalities that are to be covered by the health insurances, such as the draft of by-laws (section 11), and provisions for its administration (section 12), the allocation of the administrative costs (section 22) and sanctions in case of non-compliance (section 28).

2. Pre-paid Medicine Companies

50. Law 26682 sets forth the regulation regime of the pre-paid medicine companies, the voluntary adhesion plans, and the supplementary or upgrading plans for

26. The keeping of the filiation of the children who study and are not able to support themselves has a close relationship with the main Argentinean Civil Law. The National Civil and Commercial Code, in force since 2015, reformulated obligation of maintenance and supply of resources from the parents to their children, and incorporated s. 663, establishing that 'the parents' obligation to provide resources to the child lasts until the child is twenty-five, as long as the studies or professional training does not allow him to financially support himself independently'. Even though the age of twenty-five may seem excessive in some legislations and conceptions, it coincides with the average age a youngster in general graduates at university in Argentina. Thus, the fact that a person is entitled to health coverage for the term of the financial support by the parents- under the conditions already mentioned- goes hand in hand with this basic concept of the local Civil Law.
27. In Argentina, the trend to the legal marriage has decreased in the last years. Nevertheless, the formulae 'ostensible family treatment' used in the Health Insurance Law appears to be convenient as for example if a couple decides to live together but do not get married, one of them may add the other to the family group as long as such condition is proved – in the city of Buenos Aires- by means of the 'Cohabitation Certificate' in the Civil Registry Office.

further services which are offered by the Healthcare Providers (ASS in Spanish) under Laws 23660 and 23661. This includes cooperatives, employee-ownership trusts, civil associations, and foundations whose partial or total objective is to render services of prevention, protection, treatment, and rehabilitation of the users' health, by means of voluntary membership, through an adhesion payment system, whether that is on their own or by means of third parties related or hired to that effect, whether that be by individual or corporative agreement.

51. The scope of action of the regulation is clearly wide: the great number of individuals affected indicates a plural universe, a multifaceted market in which there exist – under the same regulation – cooperatives, pre-paid medicine companies and hybrid elements, all of them giving 'benefits of the human health prevention, protection, treatment and rehabilitation to the users', as law 26682 puts it, and tries to define the pre-paid company in its section 2: '… any and all physical or legal persons, regardless of its type, legal condition or denomination, whose objective is to render services of prevention, protection, treatment, and rehabilitation of the users' health, by means of a voluntary membership, through an adhesion payment system, whether that is on their own or by means of third parties related or hired to that effect, whether that be by individual or corporative agreement.'

52. By means of the definition, the law also specifies a dual scheme in several aspects: 'legal or physical person', 'on their own or by means of third parties related or hired to that effect' (what could be summarized as 'on their own or by means of a hired third parties'), by 'individual or corporative agreement'. The legislative technicality used to refer to any physical or legal persons 'regardless of its type, legal condition or denomination' focuses on its role to disregard any type of speculation of any person trying to operate as a pre-paid medicine company beyond the limits of the law, under another legal regime, or under non-regulated conditions. Hence, the activity is the one providing the legal context and not its denomination. This wording seems silver tongue as many entities (health insurances, mutuals, trade unions or isolated companies) which are not incorporated as pre-paid medicine companies have entered the market commercializing health plans; yet with the sole interest of rendering their services but with no intention of complying with the duties arising from the law.

53. However, in judicial instances, it has already been pointed out that even if the internal rules of a company – acting as a pre-paid – medicine enterprise or trading with health plans – expressly said that it is not a pre-paid medicine company, that will not be ground for the company to free themselves of their duties: '… it is not possible to be, by principle, in a privileged judicial situation in comparison with the rest of the health insurance plans and pre-paid medicine companies (Section 7 of the law 26682). This implies that, in the absence of a legal regulation that expressly exempt them from giving the coverage claimed, they shall perform all necessary formalities to make it effective.'[28]

54. As a minimum, the subjects involved in this regulation shall cover the Obligatory Medicine Program in force and the prevision of the Law of Disabilities (24901) together with all its amendments (section 7). The general rule is that partial coverages are not accepted, with the following exceptions: 'a) Exclusively dental services; b) Medical emergency services and people's sanitary transfers; c) those who develop their activity in only one exclusive location, with a list of users inferior to five thousand'. As regards the contract cancellation of the pre-paid medicine (section 9), it is established that the users are entitled to end the contract at any time, without limitations or penalty, having the obligation of clearly notifying this decision with a thirty-day notice. On the other hand, the pre-paid medicine companies have only two reasons for the early termination of the contract: when the user either incurs in, at least, the lack of three consecutive payments and/or has forged the affidavit. In the case of lack of payment, after the term of payment established has passed and prior to the early termination, the pre-paid medicine company or the entity operating in the terms of Law 26682 shall irrefutably communicate to the user about the payment in arrears ordering him to honour the payment within ten days of the notification.

55. In this last point, Resolution 163/2018 of the Superintendence of Health Services has intended to clarify the way in which the supplier can proceed with the early termination of a contract against a user. Section 10 of said resolution establishes that:

> In the case of THREE (3) consecutive full payments in arrears, the contract relationship is deemed to continue, and the entities shall not be entitled to terminate the contract when:
>
> (a) The company has failed to send the irrefutable notice pursuant to section 9º, paragraph 2, subsection a, of the Decree Nº 1993/2011, after THREE (3) full consecutive payments are in arrears, notwithstanding any other notification previously sent.
> (b) The policyholder pays such owed money within TEN (10) working days after the irrefutable notice afore-mentioned has been sent.
> (c) The company has failed to irrefutably communicate the termination of the contract to the policyholder and the latter has paid the THREE (3) due payments, even if he has done so after the term of the Ten (10) days provided in Section 9º, paragraph 2º, subsection a), of the Decree Nº 1993/2011.
>
> In all cases, the policyholder and his family shall keep the loyalty benefit they have in the company.

28. Case N 8311/2015 –S.I.- 'G.S., G. and Others Against Health Insurance of the National Judicial Power About Health Amparo', Room I of the Federal Civil and Commercial Court decision procedure dated on 30/10/18.

56. Another important point of the rule is that prepaid drug contracts do not have waiting periods or loopholes in the PMO, just as pre-existing conditions cannot be grounds for rejection by a company; the claim in the book is a valid reason. According to the regulations (Article 10), the application permit – the Norwegian Health Authority – is to grant permission in case of non-compliance to admit users with pre-existing health conditions for a valid reason. As with pre-existing medical conditions, age is not a reason to reject potential participants (section 11). Therefore, institutional, insurance or prepaid drug provider medical review standards cannot substitute for application approval.

57. As it was previously mentioned, the law considers two contractual modalities: the individual contract and the corporative contract. The individual one is the typical 'direct' relationship with the pre-paid medicine without intermediaries, as any other subscription to a service (however, in this case, it is a health service). Section 15 of Law 26682, does not define what a corporative contract means, but it gives an idea when granting the users the right of continuity in certain circumstances: 'The user registered through a group or corporative contract that has ended the labour relationship with the company and has signed the contract with one of the legal entities of section 1° of this law, is entitled to the continuity of the loyalty Benefit recognized in one of the plans of the legal entities mentioned in section 1 of the present law – as long as he requires it within sixty (60) days as from the termination of the labour relationship with the company or entity he was working for. The individual covered under Section 1 of the present law shall keep the Benefit of the Plan until the end of the sixty (60)-day period.'

58. From this section, it is clear that the statutes begin when, for example, a company contracts a prepaid drug company. Thus, the employer purchases a set of medical plans which are distributed among its employees. The user is the beneficiary who pays or does not pay part of the plan. In all cases, the obligated subject is the prepaid company and the beneficiary is the employee (the user). There are other types of contracts that could be called 'hybrid' because strictly speaking, they do not fall under either of the two models described in Law 26682. Perhaps the most common is enrolling someone with prepaid medication through a union-run health insurance plan: an employee has a union-run health insurance plan; and the union-run health insurance company in turn has an agreement with the prepaid drug company for a difference in fee payment, the worker can use the prepaid drug and its benefits. Thus, prepaid drugs and the health insurance fund managed by the syndicate are jointly and severally liable for the claims of the user, who finds it more convenient to enlist the services of a private provider for a fixed amount, which turns out to be cheaper than even hiring the prepaid drug plan directly.

3. Superintendence of Health Services

59. The Superintendence of Health Services – also known as the (SSSalud) – is the Authority of Application in terms of health. Created by the Decree 1615/1996, such regulation set forth that the institution should operate as a decentralized agency of the National Public Administration in the jurisdiction of the Social Action and Health Ministry with an autonomous administrative, economic, and financial regime, as a supervision, audit and control agency of the providers conforming the National Healthcare System.

60. Decree 1547/2007 approved the organization's structure of the SSSalud, with ten main objectives:

(1) To regulate and supervise Health Services, to ensure policies compliance in the area; to promote, preserve and recover the population's health, striking the balance among the users, service providers, and financial institutions in a context of free competition, transparency, economic efficiency, and social equity.
(2) To provide the legal framework to regulate the development of the institutions' control and regulation activities.
(3) To control the operation of the union-run health insurance providers system, those of the intervening providers and those of any other supplier or financial institution of medical-assistant services included.
(4) To approve entry applications to the institutions´ system and to promote the intervention thereof to ensure the continuity and normalization of the health service.
(5) To approve the Medical Services Program and the Resources and Expenses Funding for its implementation.
(6) To guarantee and promote the beneficiary's free election and effective access to the health insurance.
(7) To annually report the Institution's activities in a Public Hearing.
(8) To perform a compliance control of the Institution's ethical obligations as well as those of their dependencies and to develop control mechanisms and processes against fraud and corruption.
(9) To check the efficiency and efficacy of the Health Service Superintendence's Strategic Plan and the annual operative plans thereof as well as to develop corrective actions to optimize the expected results.
(10) To negotiate the labour bargaining agreements.

61. Resolution 1379/2010 of the Superintendence of Health Services established a set of punishments for those failing to comply with the regulations on health (insurance providers and suppliers registered in the National Registry of Providers) Thus, the punishments as follows are set forth for the Healthcare Providers: (a) Warning; (b) penalty; (c) intervention; and (d) registration cancelation of the National Health Insurances Registry. (Decree 576/93 PEN., Annex II, section 42). For the Providers registered in the National Registry of Providers, it is provided: (a) registration suspension up to one year from the National Registry of Providers and (b) registration cancellation from the National Registry of Providers. The penalties for registration suspensions and cancellations in the National Registry of Providers shall be valid for all insurance providers.

62. The truth is the punishment scheme is one of the greatest debts of the Superintendence of Health Services, because even though there are countless administrative files against default Insurance Providers, the fact that this agency is used so often without further consequences for the health insurers and drug companies prepaid, speaks clearly of the scarce penalty rigor and of the quasi-testimonial role played by the Superintendence on this aspect. This makes the sanctions visible only because they are not strictly enacted or applied, without consequences for the lenders, which constitutes the great failure of the institution: neither to establish exemplary sanctions nor to have the tools and mechanisms to enforce the rules that they themselves have drawn up to respect. Users' claims usually end up in court, as the Superintendence of Health Services is not a useful tool for them, if not – at best – an endorsement of a violation of rights.

4. Consumer Protection Act

63. It is worth mentioning that consumer protection legislation has attracted particular interest in recent years and has gained ground and importance since the mid-1990s, especially in relation to medical law. Although he is still too young and has inherited the pillars of Anglo-Saxon law, whose capitalist tradition has meant that it dictates clear rules for the protection of users, consumer law is made up of a diversified and generous regulatory framework and at the same time covers all types of dispute in which a natural or legal person who uses services or goods for free or for a fee as an end user intervenes for his own benefit or that of his family or social group. Also noteworthy is the importance of the local courts, which have gradually expanded the range of action of consumers and created more and more certainties for the weaker contracting party: there is practically no place where a consumer right can be asserted that consumer law not to intervene; moreover there an increasing conviction that the consumer has to be protected and that that protection must be guaranteed by the States and its structure.

64. In point II.a.i. we have already seen the predominant role given to the consumers' right 'in terms of protecting their health, security and economic interests' among other privileges the user is given, guaranteed by the National Constitution – the Magna Carta – in its amendment in 1994. However, the notion of consumerism transcends the National Constitution. Even Law 24240 was created before the amendment and was supplemented by a series of fundamental laws that demonstrate the role of the consumer and, to a large extent, the privileged position of those who interact with him, which implies greater accountability, particularly in the right to health is at stake.

65. Law 24240, enacted on 22 September 1993, form the necessary ground for consumption relationships. First, it provides concrete definitions such as for example about the providers (section 2 of Law 24240): legal or physical persons of public or private nature, professionally developing activities of production, montage, creation, construction, transformation, importation, trademark license, distribution and commercialization of goods and services, intended to consumers or users even on an occasional basis. Beyond this definition – thus excepted from compliance of the law herein – there are the services of freelance professionals who must have a university certificate or degree and professional license given by officially recognized professional associations or authority with the power thereto. If subject to this law, all marketing is done about the rendering of such a product or service.

66. The interpretation of the section has brought about long debates and discussions, especially in relation to its scope and the liable parties. Chapter II of the Law 24240, entitled 'Information to the consumers and their health protection', is clear about the value of this rule closely related to the sanitary context. In this sense, the law establishes that 'the provider is bound to give the consumer whatever is related to the basic characteristics of the goods and services they provide, and commercialization conditions in a clear, detailed and accurate way' (section 4). The text further sets forth that 'the information must be provided free of charge in a physical way and has to be clear enough to be understood by the user. The means of communication in a physical way shall be replaced provided that the user or consumer clearly chooses an alternative means that the provider should make available for him.'

67. Furthermore, the law affirms that the goods and services must be supplied or rendered in such a way that, when used in normal and foreseeable conditions they do not represent a hazard to the consumers' health or physical integrity (section 5) and that 'the good and services included in the public services at home, whose utilization would entail a risk for the consumers' health or physical integrity, must be commercialized respecting the mechanisms, instructions, and rules reasonable or established to guarantee the safety thereof' (section 6), giving, to that end, a manual about the use, installation and maintenance in the national language.

68. In addition to the health protection provisions on the use of services hired or products purchased, the Law 24240 deserves special attention and further reading about the relationships between the beneficiary and the pre-paid medicine companies or the union-administered health insurance companies. In consideration of the excesses incurred in by the latter – that in many cases have a domineering position in the market and in the health system, the consecrated underpinnings in the Consumer Protection Act become more and more relevant. Among the duties already mentioned in terms of information under section 4; and of safety and protection under sections 5 and 6, the following should be further considered:

(1) *Humane treatment.* Section 8 bis establishes that the providers shall guarantee conditions of assistance and humane and equal treatment for the consumers and users and abstain from behaving in a way that may place the latter in a shameful, intimidating or vexatious condition. Nor can they make a difference to foreign consumers in terms of price, technical or commercial quality or in any other way with respect to the goods and services they offer; a logical imperative, if it is assumed that to do otherwise, would involve discriminatory treatment. Any exception to this rule must be approved by the competent authority for valid reasons of public interest. This humane treatment also means that in the event of an out-of-court complaint, no means can be used

which gives the appearance of a judicial complaint. Otherwise, the fault of the non-compliant subject will result in a penalty, a fine and the corresponding right to compensation from the consumer.

The justice has clearly harboured this principle in the relationships between the consumer and the provider of medical services. For example, it has been said that 'the unilateral direct termination of the contract by the pre-paid medicine company due to the sole consideration of a single medical certificate and an arbitrary accusation of falseness in the completion of the affidavit reveals a serious underestimation of the claimant's right. The null and void evidence of the postulated defence presented by the claimant in this process finally confirmed this hypothesis and proved, in retrospect, that the abrupt termination of the business relationship had no ground and entailed a serious indifference and rebuke of the consumer's rights, failing to observe and keep the promise of a humane treatment (Sections 1, 2, 8 bis and concordant, Law 24240)'; moreover, 'the company´s misbehaviour was not an exceptional case in isolation, but the perfect example of a wide range of conflicts in which the pattern of behaviour has once and again been verified.'[29]

(2) *Prohibition to upfront collection of money*. Section 10 quarter establishes the prohibition of 'prior notice collection of money, month in advance or any other concept, from the part of the providers, public services at home included in case of a beneficiary's request of discontinuance of the service, whether that be in person, by phone, by e-mail, or otherwise.' This protects, among other assumptions, the consumer from being forced to honour payments in arrears in case he wishes to discontinue the service (this in turn puts a stop to the collection of further interests and the claim of future fees).

(3) *Interpretation of the contract*. Section 37 extolled the fundamental principle of the Argentinean Consumption Law, common thread replicated in other social plexuses. Therefore, it is established that notwithstanding the validity of the contract, the following shall not be deemed agreed upon: 'a) the clauses denaturalizing the obligations or limiting the liability for damages; b) the clauses implying the weaver or restriction in the consumer's rights or the widening of the other party's rights; c) the clauses that provides the shifting the burden of the proof against the consumer.' Furthermore, the contract must be interpreted in the interest of the consumer and, in case of doubt as to the extent of his obligations, the lightest burden lies with the user, who is generally the weaker and less experienced. Thus is conclusive the application of the principle according to which the user is entitled, in the event of breach of the obligation of good faith, to inform or protect the legal capacity or loyalty towards the consumer, to invoke the nullity of the contract or a contract or several clauses thereof. In the event of partial nullity, the regulations instruct the judge to merge the entire contract, if necessary.

The Argentine judiciary has reaffirmed this principle in disputes with healthcare professionals and private medical service providers where the user's interests are at stake. In the event of tariff increases due to age – not authorized by

29. Case 'Gastiarena, Daiana against Omint S.A. de Servicios about Damages /// Civil and Commercial Court of Appeals, Room II, Mar del Plata, Buenos Aires, 10/10/2019'.

the Superintendence of Health Services – and therefore illegitimate and against the law – taking into account the characteristics of the prepaid drug contract, being the predetermined clauses that arise from the discipline of the hiring of the services, 'It is obvious to conclude that the clauses of the contract empowering the medical company to impose additional fees due to the age are to be deemed abusive, pursuant to sections 37 and 38 of the Law 24240, and are impinging at the same time against section 42 of the National Constitution which grants the consumers the right to the protection of their health, security and economic interests as well as equal and humane treatment.'[30] The magistrates' decision considers that 'clauses like this are to be deemed as not written, any time they affect the user's right to health, denaturalize the contract by depriving the beneficiary of the corresponding assistance whenever he is not able to pay the increment. Thus, the increase should be disregarded under section 37 of the Consumer Protection Act, since it establishes not to be deemed as written those clauses entailing the weaver or restriction of the consumers' rights, or the widening of the counterpart's rights.'

Several judgments relating to the interpretation of the contract in favour of the consumer have confirmed these criteria. Considering again the previous example, an increase in contributions due to a change in age, without the approval of the requesting authority, it was specified that 'in the activity of the union-run health insurance plans, an projection of the social security principles that have an integral nature and force to consider the controversies originated for its operation with criteria not disregarding its own objectives is to be considered (Section 14 bis, National Constitution). In this sense, it is obvious that the non-authorized increase of the fees the members pay to the health service causes an imbalance in the contract conditions favouring the strongest party of the relationships, in detriment of the weakest party's right to health and life. Hence, the pre-emptive protections are especially relevant since it is aimed at going against this vulnerability condition, structural weakness in which the user is in their relationship with the pre-paid medicine company.'[31]

(4) *Accession contract.* Also known as 'contract in forms'. Section 38 of the law 24240 affirms that the Authority of Application shall control that the accession contracts or similar will not contain abusive clauses or rebuked one by the regulations, as it is set forth pursuant to section 37. 'The same power shall be exercised upon uniform, general, standardized clauses of the contract done in forms, in templates and in general when such clauses have been unilaterally drafted and decided by the provider of the good or service, without the other party having the possibility of discussing its content', the norm also establishes amongst other things.

30. Case 'B.A.E against Omint SA about/ Ordinary Proceeding' dated on 9/5/2013; National Commercial Court Room 'C'; National Federal Administrative Court of Appeals (CNACAF), Room II, 'Medicus SA against Secretary of Commerce' dated on 8/10/1996 and most recently 'ALBAMONTE, ANA ROSA against SWISS MEDICAL SA about AMPARO', case 2496/2017, ruling dated on 09/09/19, National Civil Court nº 14, decision ratified by the Court of Appeals.
31. Case entitled 'G., E. D. and others against Swiss Medical S.A. Speedy trial about Health'/// National Federal Civil and Commercial Court of Appeals, Room III, 15/07/2020.

Once again, the Argentinean case law has shed light in this sense. Without losing sight of the previous examples – increase in the fee of the pre-paid medicine without proper approval from the SSSalud, it has been established that 'the pre-paid medical services, or health insurance contract, as it is commonly known, is invested with the characteristics of an undetermined, randomized accession contract with predisposed clauses; thus provisions under the Consumer Protection Act n° 24240 are to be applicable … it has already been said that the unilaterality of a decision taken by the stronger party as one of the main elements of the agreement (the price) inevitably implies the abusive transfer of the risk to the user … In the same vein is the provision in the National Civil and Commercial Code oriented when establishing that the rules stipulating the consumption relationships shall be construed and applied pursuant to the principle of the consumer's protection and access to sustainable consumption; thus prevailing the interpretation most favourable to the consumer (Section 1094); moreover, in case of doubts about the scope of its obligation, the least cumbersome for the consumer shall be adopted (Section 1095); the provision under Section 1119 further establishes that the clause, whether or not individually negotiated, effectively causes a significant imbalance between the rights and obligations of the parties, being the user the most prejudiced, is considered abusive.'[32]

(5) *Celerity, simplicity, obligation of collaboration from the strongest party and gratuity in favour of the consumer.* Under the title 'Rules of the process', section 53 of the law 24240 establishes that in the cases initiated due to the exercise of the consumers' rights, 'the rules of the speediest processes of the competent ordinary court jurisdiction shall govern, unless – at the party's request, the judge by means of a well-funded resolution and based on the complexity of the pretension, may deem necessary a most suitable procedure.' Therefore, for example, the process called 'Speedy' – in Chapter II of Tittle III of the Civil and Commercial Procedural Code of the Nation (CPCNN) – would give a fast way to solve a claim about consumption against a pre-paid medicine company or a union-run health insurance plan.[33] Nonetheless, due to the typical issues and urgency surrounding the conflicts in which a person's health is at stake, the claims in this sense are usually dealt with as an amparo,

32. Of the quoted ruling 'ALBAMONTE, ANA ROSA against SWISS MEDICAL SA about AMPARO', case 2496/2017, in the Room J of the Civil Court when ratifying the decision of the original jurisdiction. The same decision process corresponds to these valuable precedents: National Civil Court (CNCiv)., Room 'G', in case entitled 'M., M. A. against S. M. S.A. about amparo' – File N° 5459/2017/CA2, dated on 05/08/19. Similarly, National Civil Court (CNCiv) Room 'A', in case entitled 'M., F. H. against OMINT S.A. de servicios about amparo' – File N° 1.368/2016/CA1- dated on14/07/17.

33. It should be noted that in the speedy trial, according to the Code, all procedural terms are three days– except for the exceptions contained in s. 498 of the mentioned code-, whereas the generic term of the ordinary processes is five days (s. 150 Civil and Commercial Procedural Code of the Nation -CPCCN); here the agility of the speedy trial is to be highlighted.

whose regime – Law 16986 at a national level – is even faster than a speedy process since the terms are hours[34] and process implies a shorter deployment in comparison with the ordinary one.

69. Furthermore, this section seeks to provide consumers with some edge in the context of excessive formalism, when establishing that those initiating the actions pursuant to Law 24240 'representing an individual's right or interest, shall be entitled to show proof by means power of attorney under the terms and conditions established in the norm.' The regulation clearly establishes that 'the person shall show proof by means of the corresponding public instrument or power of attorney signed by the giver certified by judicial or police authority or public attorney', or else show proof by means of a simple power certified by the Authority of Application who shall confirm the principal's identity and address and the appointment, identity, address, and signature of the representative thereof.

70. An important issue, also in favour of the consumer and his interests, is the fact that the supplier has the duty to 'contribute to the process any and all evidence that he may possess according to the characteristics of the goods or services, and to be at all times willing to help to solve the subject matter of the case'. Following this precept and to the light of the example previously taken, a pre-paid medicine company should present in any dispute the contract subscribed together with the user, the terms of such a commitment, the documents modifying the relationship and all instruments useful to clarify any confusing situation or the truth being sought after.

71. Finally, this chapter outlines the benefits of free legal advice in relation to proceedings brought under applicable law for personal interests or rights. However, it grants the defendant the opportunity to choose to prove the consumer's creditworthiness by preliminary issue, which might stop the benefit of gratuity. It is noteworthy that this benefit of free legal advice is comparable but not equal to the benefit of waiver of court fees and costs provided under Title II, Chapter VI of the CPCNN (which entails the initiation of an independent trial, yet annexed to a main conflict, with periods to produce evidence and a different process). According to case law, the benefit of free legal advice stipulated by the Consumers' Protection laws refers to all financial burdens, including judicial costs, and neither the requirement of poverty nor any additional proof other than the capacity to be a consumer is required for its granting. The only requirement is that the law that governs the dispute must have its origin in the regulations established for the protection of consumers.[35]

34. A case in point: the appeal remedy against the final judgment of amparo pursuant to law n° 16986, should be lodged 'within 48 hours of the notification of the contested resolution and must be well—funded, having to be overruled or sustained within the 48 hours' (s. 15, Law 16986). Nonetheless, it should be admitted that in the custom of the courts '48 hours' means 'two days', even though it is not the same in relation to terms.

35. Case 'Holzwarth Patricia against Caja de Seguros S.A. about damages-contract non-compliance', Room 1 of the Civil and Commercial Court of Appeals n° 2 in La Plata, Buenos Aires; decision dated on 22 Apr. 2021.

72. Other laws and resolutions that firmly strengthen the advantages of the relationship's least advantageous party have accelerated the advancement of the Law of Consumption in terms of health in addition to the clauses in the National Constitution of Argentina and the Consumer Protection Act regarding users. For example, Resolution 139/2020 of the Domestic Commerce Secretariat (under the frame of the Productive Development Ministry) about the notion of 'hyper-vulnerable consumers' and the need to preserve them. The idea of the consumer itself arises from understanding the user as a vulnerable subject against another contracting party that is, in many cases, a company with more tools and information than the user itself. The universe of hyper-vulnerable consumers is supposed to receive from the National State 'a prioritized assistance by means of the implementation of personalized, dynamic, and agile strategies to allow a right settlement for the disputes according to each case's needs', pursuant to the norms in case of claims and emergences of a determined group.

73. Resolution 139/2020 defines the term 'hyper-vulnerable consumers' as those people who are 'in vulnerable conditions due to their age, gender, physical or mental condition or else social, economic, ethnic and/or cultural conditions, causing certain difficulties to fully exercise their rights as consumers.' This definition is already elaborated in the first paragraph of this title. When claiming that non-profit legal organizations target the groups covered by this definition as legal hyper-vulnerable persons, an exception is taken into account. Hence, causes of hyper vulnerability are considered as follows:

(a) claims involving children and teenagers' rights;
(b) individuals belonging to the collective+ Lesbians, Gays, Bisexuals, and Transgender (LGBT);
(c) individuals over 70 years of age;
(d) individuals with a disability having the corresponding certificate;
(e) migrants or tourists;
(f) individuals belonging to indigenous communities;
(g) sub-urbanity;
(h) residents in popular areas pursuant to Law N° 27453;
(i) socioeconomic vulnerable conditions such as:
    (1) Being a pensioner or retiree or a worker under a contract of employment who receives a gross salary equal or minor to TWO (2) minimum average salaries.
    (2) Being self-employed and registered in the category whose annual salary by month is not more than TWO (2) times the minimum average salary.
    (3) Being beneficiary of a non-contributed pension and receiving a gross by month income not higher than TWO (2) times the minimum average salary.
    (4) Being beneficiary of a Pregnancy Subsidy for Social Protection and Universal Childcare Subsidy for Social Protection.
    (5) Being registered in the Social Self-employed Regime.
    (6) Being registered in the Special Regime of Social Security for Domestic Employees (Law 26844).
    (7) Getting unemployment benefits.

(8) Being entitled to a wartime 'Atlántico Sur' veterans' pension (Law N° 23848).

74. It can be deduced from the list that the idea of a 'hyper-vulnerable consumer' is compatible with the pressing demands regarding health. In this regard, among other types of users, children, teenagers, seniors, people with disabilities, people living in suburban neighbourhoods, and pensioners are, to a large extent, the neglected parties or the leaders of the subjugation of their rights when requiring access to the sanitary system (due to lack of income, resources, due to the need of excessively costly treatments which are unknown by the medical coverage). Therefore, the introduction of this Resolution in the health industry helps frame and highlight the need for a special protection for consumers, and even, a special treatment, since in these cases, even the information must be provided using a clear, accessible, concise, and colloquial language that the receiver can understand; furthermore, the providers must be collaborative and tend to guarantee the suitable and quick settlement of the dispute, being willing to solve the matter with immediacy. These two main principles (accessible language and willingness to help) are also provided in the ministerial Resolution 139/2020.

75. The Civil and Commercial Code of the Nation – valid since August 2015 – has also sealed the importance of the consumers' law. Title III under this Code deals with the contracts of consumption, consecrating the guidelines already seen in the legislation. Therefore, it confirms the interpretation of the agreement in the sense most favourable for the consumer (section 1094 and 1095 of the Civil and Commercial Code of the Nation), the obligation of humane treatment towards the user (section 1097) and the equal and non-discriminatory treatment (section 1098), the duty to inform (section 1100), the regime of abusive clauses (sections 1118 and 1119), among other notions, the interest of the user which must always be first.

III. Financing of the Healthcare System

76. As it has already been said, the Argentinean Health System is composed of three sectors: the public one (The State), the private one (such as pre-paid medicine companies) and the social security (union-run health insurance plans). The way to funding them is different in every case.

A. The Public Sector

77. In the case of the public sector, it is noteworthy that the National State obtains its revenue from the taxes, asset sales, financing operations and other modalities. According to the official information, in the year 2020, Argentina Peso (ARS) 5,981,986.34, (in millions of pesos) were collected, 94.60% of the total forecasted. The areas of the highest revenue were tax revenue (2,669,878.66), property income (1,794,175.22) and withholding and contributions (1,318,698.16). The budget of the National Health Ministry (and its dependent agencies) was ARS

73,779.30 million pesos for the year 2020 at the very beginning, and later it rose to ARS 167,782,38 (a 1.30% of the total updated credit): in that year, 95.05% of that last amount was executed, a year that was characterized by uncertainty due to a pandemic which reorganized the map of the local health and its resources. The income's peak percentage went for the pharmaceutical and medication expenditure representing 22.76% of the total budget.[36]

78. Attention should be drawn to the fact that only during 2020, transfers were budgeted to the private sector for a total of United States Dollar (USD) 55,214.69 million to finance present-day expenditures (including transfers 'without justification', to different non-profit organizations, social help and scholarships); further transfers were made to provincial and municipal administrations to finance current expenditures for a total of USD 30,425.49 million (the allocations to such jurisdictions, as Capital expenditure ascended to USD 726.93 million); transfers to overseas (international organizations such as the Pan-American Health Organization and the Iberia-American Social Security Organization to finance current expenses) were equal to USD 9.76 million, among other transfers which are clear examples of the inter-relation among the three sectors. In addition to the budget allocated to the Ministry of Health, there are expenses for the health system that are not foreseen by the Ministry. Therefore, considering the same period in 2020, the National Social Security Administration has a budget of USD 82,701.59 million for transfers and contributions to social security or decentralized institutions; the budget allocated to these institutions under the supervision of the Health Service is 35,688.45 US dollars for financial assistance to healthcare providers and others.

79. It must be stressed that the Law of Pre-paid medicine under section 5 gives the Authority of Application the obligation of controlling the payment of the benefits given and billed to public hospitals or any other institution of the national, provincial or municipal public sector; which implies not a way of financing but rather a compensation in favour of the public sector when the user receives assistance in the public sector even having, for example, a pre-paid medicine plan.

B. Private Sector

80. The main funding source of the pre-paid medicine plans is the users' monthly payment of the fees. The fee of each plan cannot be freely fixed without any criteria by the companies; in fact, The law of re-paid medicine (26682) establishes that the authority of application shall, among other things, authorize and control the models of contracts entered into between the providers and the users in all the modalities of agreement and plans, aside from authorizing and revising the value of the fee and their adjustments proposed by the pre-paid medicine companies.

36. SOURCE https://www.presupuestoabierto.gob.ar/sici/de-donde-vienen-los-recursos.

81. By the same token, Decree 66/2019 established that the fees the users pay shall be authorized pursuant to the provisions set forth under section 17 of the pre-paid medicine law. The companies that intent to increase the amount of the fee the users pay, shall individually present the request to the SUPERINTENDENCE OF HEALTH SERVICES and the latter shall inform its decision within forty-five days from the presentation of the request before the SSSalud, to file the petition with the Health Ministry.

82. Section 17 of the law 26682 is conclusive when precising that the Authority of Application shall control and guarantee the reasonability of the fees of the benefit plans, authorizing the increase when that increment is based on variations in the costs structure and on the risk actuarial reasonable calculation. As another example of increased fee requirements, it follows from the statute that private sector service providers can set price differences for schemes by age group at the time of contract, no more than three (3) times between the first and last age group. This means that the price difference should be determined when the user enters the system, and not during the duration of the contract, which is repeatedly emphasized by judicial practice and the same application authority. As from Decree 66/2019, the charges based on age were established, if this was provided in the agreement; something that has brought about a debate yet to be unravelled since the former criteria were opposed to the pretension of the companies that wish to make such increases.

C. Union-run Health Insurance Plans

83. Law 23660 establishes that Union-run health insurance plans shall allocate their resources primarily to health benefits (section 3) and shall be liable to allocate at least 80% of the gross resources deducted from the Redistribution Solidarity Fund created in the jurisdiction of the National Healthcare Administration (ANSSAL in Spanish),[37] to the health services rendering established by the insurance to their beneficiaries (section 5). The same section stipulates that the Union-run health insurance plans gathering revenues in a centralized way shall allocate 70% of the earnings in each jurisdiction to meet the health needs of their beneficiaries residing in such jurisdiction. Moreover, they shall guarantee, under the regulations, regional solidarity redistribution mechanisms ensuring access from the part of the beneficiaries to the health services without any discrimination whatsoever.

84. The core of the financing is in section 16 of the law 23660 where the resulting contributions for the support of the actions to be performed by the union-run health insurance plans are established: (a) a contribution equal to 6% of the workers' wage under a contract of employment, the employer's contribution to the union-run health insurance system (this pursuant to section 80m of the law 25565); (b) a contribution from the employees under a contract of employment equal to 3% of

37. The ANSSAL, created by law n° 23661, after the merger with National Bureau of Health Insurances (DINOS in Spanish) and the National Institute of Health Insurances (INOS in Spanish), constitutes the current authority of application.

their salary. Furthermore, 1.5% of his salary will be paid for each qualifying family dependent (primary and co-habitant family members of the policyholder who ostensibly have a family status shall be entitled to have the health insurance of the employee); (c) in the case of the State-owned partnership or companies, the contribution for the health insurance support cannot be inferior, in a constant currency, to the average of the last twelve months prior to the enactment of the present law.

85. This section also reminds us that the contributions paid by pensioners and the various methods for financing healthcare, established by laws, decrees, collective agreements or other special regulations, remain valid. Moreover, 'current amounts, and/or fixed contributions established in collective bargaining agreements or in any other provisions higher than the ones in the present law shall keep in force; as well as other resources of a different nature in charge of the same parties or third parties, for the financing and administration of the union-run health insurance plans.'

86. The main purpose of the already mentioned Solidarity Distribution Fund is to give subsidies, loans, and funding to the insurance providers, to be able to give the system's beneficiaries the basic medical assistance benefits to guarantee their health, pursuant to the Decree 1081/89. The Superintendence of Health Services is the one in charge of implementing, regulating, and managing the resources of such Fund, in urgent need of helping the insurance providers because of the high-economic impact benefits or those demanding an extended coverage in time. Again: This is about maintaining equity and fairness in healthcare, which is the foundation of a system designed to avoid discrimination and address coverage gaps for users regardless of industry. Therefore, the state undertakes to help the insurer – with regard to certain benefits – so that it does not go bankrupt or end up in a difficult financial situation if it has to pay expensive benefits.

87. By the same token, Resolution 1200/2012 of the SSSalud created the Unique Reimbursement System (SUR in Spanish), to strengthen the health insurance providers' financing in case of low-incidence medical benefits, high-economic impact ones and those of extended treatments, a system that during 2020 made transfers to the insurance providers for the total of $23,855,742,705.98.

88. Finally, another backing to the health insurance plans is the Automatic Nominative Subsidy of the union-run health insurance plans ('SANO' in Spanish, with all the provisions of the Decree N° 1901/2006), that as described by the SSSa lud,[38] grants the beneficiary entities of the system, a minimum contribution per user, to cover the medical assistance benefits. This subsidy considers the calculation of the expense based on the demographic group with similar epidemiological characteristics, avoiding the selection of risk, since the fixing of the fee related to the benefit prevents discrimination and guarantees accessibility to the system. This distribution model considers, among other parameters, the total amount of beneficiaries in the Health Insurance Providers, including the families of the workers.

38. https://www.sssalud.gob.ar/index.php?page=bus_os_sub.

§3. Sources of Medical Law

89. As it has been elaborated so far, Argentinean Health Law in an emerging branch that has gained robustness in the last decades, has been affected by the successive economic crises (which have brought about lack of coverage from the part of those liable to ensure the members' welfare), the re-valuation of the consumer's role in the society, the detriment suffered by some sectors and the expansion of rights in healthcare. Nowadays, the National Constitution, the international Treaties subscribed by Argentina, the set of rules which is the basis for the pre-paid medicine companies and the union-run health insurance plans and the special regulations applicable to each case help us fully understand Medical Law. Let´s keep in mind that the Argentinean system establishes a minimum coverage (PMO) and not a ceiling, a status of equality and equity always to be considered, regardless of the person's socioeconomic condition.

90. Different from other branches of law, resolutions by the Superintendence of Health Services and even more: case laws are of relevance. The doctrine is also making its contribution and therefore it has become compulsory to read and study rulings to have a complete map of regulations of the Health Law in Argentina. The lack of a specific code and of a Branch specially dedicated to health completes the fragmentation of the system.

Part I. The Medical Profession

Chapter 1. Access to the Medical Profession

§1. Training of Physicians

91. Argentina has a variety of public and private institutions where one can study medicine. Among the public, we can mention: Universidad of Buenos Aires (UBA), National University of La Plata (UNLP), National University of Cuyo (UNCUYO) National University of La Matanza (UNLAM). Among the private institutions there are Pontificia Universidad Católica Argentina (UCA) Santa María de los Buenos Aires, Austral University, Morón University (UM), H.A. Barceló Foundation.

92. According to the data given by Federal Observatory of Human Resources in Health in the year 2020[39] (OFERHUS) – based on the information given by the Bureau of University Statistics of the National Ministry of Education, between 2007 and 2018, the number of new students in the course of studies of medicine exponentially increased; however, this was the case for the graduates. Hence, in the year 2007, there were 10,532 new students and only 5,139 graduates in 2008, 10,900 new students and 5,549 graduates. Until 2015, there was a steady growth among the applicants (16,837) whereas the number of graduates continued decreasing in a smaller proportion (4,421). As from the year 2016, the number of new students soared up to 23,207, whereas the figure in the case of the graduates remained practically the same (4,422). In 2017, the number of new students again augmented (28,237) while the number of graduates was just 4,864. The last official data revealed that by 2018, the number of new students kept rising to get to 28,912, while the number of graduates was 5,075. If we compare the numbers of new students and graduates in 2007 with those of 2018, the contrast is startling.

93. If we compare other courses of study in the sciences of health and based on another study by OFERHUS,[40] between the years 2008 and 2015 Medicine was the

39. https://www.argentina.gob.ar/salud/oferhus/datos/formaciongrado/medicina.
40. Source https://www.argentina.gob.ar/sites/default/files/oferhus._la_formacion_de_grado_y_posgrado_en_argentina._ano_2017.pdf.

second course of study with the highest number of new students year by year,[41] just below psychology – from 15,733 of new students in 2008 to 18,978 in 2015 – and just over Kinesiology – 6,719 new students until 2015, Odontology – 3,365 in the same period, Biochemistry – 2,591 also in 2015, and Pharmacy 1,705 new students – the only course of study of the ones herein mentioned that registered a drop in the number of new students, as in the year 2008 it had been of 2,009. In the case of the graduates, the trend in other courses of study is like that of medicine. According to the findings of the study, the decline in the number of medical graduates by 2015 could correspond to the opening of new courses in recent years, which have not yet shown the first number of graduates.

94. Among the institutions where to study medicine, the best is University of Buenos Aires (UBA), which in the year 2021 was considered the best one in Ibero America for the seventh time, concurrently reaching 69th place worldwide in the Quacquarelli Symonds (QS) ranking – among approximately 24 thousand universities, a standing that has been maintained throughout the years, registering a 'steady improvement in the international evaluations' and being 'the unique public, massive, research-intensive and free university in positions of excellence' according to a report of the institution itself.[42] In the UBA, medicine is part of the graduate curricula, with no entrance exam (different from other universities) with a duration of approximately seven years, divided into four stages: Ciclo Básico Común (CBC), (common program for all courses of studies in the UBA, which roughly takes one year to be completed and is available in specific places, not in the facilities of the school of medicine), the Biomedical Stage (which is attended in the main building of the school of medicine placed in 2155 Paraguay St, in Buenos Aires city), the Clinical Stage (which is attended in the School and in different University hospitals or hospitals associated to the School) and the Rotating Annual Internship (taking place in the Hospital Teaching Training Unit).

95. Considering UBA as an example, the physicians' formation goes in ascending order from the generalization to the specialization. Hence, the beginning is the CBC lasting two semesters with three subjects each. Once these courses have been passed, students can access the Faculty of Medicine where they begin the Biomedical Internship lasting two and a half years. Based on the institution's objectives, this educational phase aims to help the student understand the structure and function of a biologically, psychologically and socially healthy human being. In this stage, the student begins to absorb knowledge of anatomy, embryology, mental health, histology and cell biology. The following stage – the Clinical one – also takes two and a half years. The main objective is for the student to be able to prevent, diagnose, and establish treatment and rehabilitation schemes for several pathologies and the five

41. There are differences in the official information in this aspect, even when that information was collected and analysed by the same source (OFERHUS) which reported that in 2015, the course of studies in medicine registered 16,081 new registered students, whereas -as it was previously expressed-in another report in the same year, the Observatory registered 16,837 new students. Despite this difference, the context of the situation is still the same in relation to the place that the course of studies in medicine is positioned in Argentina.
42. http://www.uba.ar/noticia/20233.

most important subjects and their specializations are studied: Medical Clinics, Paediatrics, Surgery, Psychiatry, and Gynaecology; and the other hand, Public Health, Mental Health, Legal Medicine and Primary Health Assistance. In the case of UBA, in the Clinical Stage, the educational model based on tutoring is implemented with teacher – service rendering integration.

96. Finally, the Rotating Annual Internship (IAR) has a total number of 2,140 horas, distributed in the following way: thirty-two weeks in the hospital assigned form Monday to Friday from 8 to 2 PM to finish the modules established in this stage; 844 hours of duty and 528 hours devoted to obligatory curricula activities related to the technical specialty of each of the modules of the IAR. Upon completion of this stage, the student is able to sit for the final exam of the Clinical Stage. This final stage in the course is focused on the practical application of the knowledge acquired in the two previous stages with the corresponding supervision so that the student can have the clinical criteria and go further in their skills. Thus, the physician-to-be is incorporated into hospital and extra hospital working teams, a model similar to the medical residence (which is also available in the country in the case of specializations of recent graduates). In this way, the future healthcare professional can also gain experience in the exchange with the patient and his family with appropriate guidance.

§2. Manpower Planning

I. Freedom of Establishment

97. The Constitution of Argentina guarantees all inhabitants the right to 'work and practise any and all legal industry' (section 14), which includes that of the health profession. However, this freedom does not imply deregulation (*see* 'Chapter 2. The practice of medicine') since the State has the obligation and the responsibility of verifying the technical skills and the ethical behaviour of certain professions such as for example that of the physicians. In fact, Argentina has abundant legislation in that sense, with a special interest in all aspects concerning sanitary work for the population. The powers of the State are also linked to the internal regulations of the various professions via professional associations. Health administration and regulation of professional practice in the health sector are in the hands of the individual federal states, so approval procedures are carried out by local ministries. Some federal states delegate the licensing of certain healthcare professions to professional associations.

98. According to an official study drafted by Federal Observatory of Human Resources in Health (OFERHUS) based on data from the Federal Network of Professional Health Registries (REFEPS)[43] from April 2020,[44] until mid-2019, in

43. The Federal Network of Healthcare Professionals Registries (REFEPS by its acronym in Spanish) has contained the updated information regarding the licensed professionals in all the jurisdictions in the country available in the Integrated System of Argentinean Sanitary Information (SISA by its

Argentina, there were 182,189 physicians, which represents 40.5 physicians every ten thousand inhabitants. The number is great if compared to other countries. According to the information gathered by World Health Organization (WHO),[45] in 2017 there were 23.3 physicians for every ten thousand inhabitants in the region of the Americas, being this number even higher than the European countries, that altogether have 33.8 professionals in medicine every ten thousand inhabitants.

§3. Licensing of Physicians

I. General Practitioners

99. In Argentina, it is necessary to complete higher education to obtain a diploma and be part of a healthcare team. By ministerial resolution N°6 dated 13 January 1997, for a degree to be officially recognized it must have two basic requirements: the total number of hours of the curriculum must be 2600 in on-site modality and that number of hours is to be at least distributed in four academic years. There are two laws which regulate the graduate's formation: on the one hand, the National Education Law (N°26.206/06), which elaborates the regulations of the National Education System in the public and private institutions; on the other hand, the National Higher Education Law (N°24521/95), which sets forth specific regulations for high formation institutions whether they are university or not.

100. The last law mentioned covers all institutions whether they are national, provincial, municipal, public, or private. Section 43 of that law, without being explicitly mentioned, covers all professions related to health: Pharmacy, Biochemistry, Medicine, Odontology, Psychology, Veterinary, Biomedical Engineering, Nursing, Speech therapy, Kinesiology, Nutrition and Obstetrics. The same section also specifies certain requirements in the training process of these professions. In terms of curricula, they must comply with the criteria established by the Ministry of Education and Culture; in relation to the courses mentioned, they must periodically be credited by the National Commission for University Evaluations and Accreditations (CONEAU) or by private entities recognized and authorized to that end. The CONEAU is a decentralized body dedicated to improving the quality of university training. With this in mind, they draw up evaluation regulations and methods of accrediting programs of study. This commission is placed under the supervision of the Ministry of National Education.

101. Section 43 of the Higher Education Law establishes the control of the syllabus, the periodic accreditation, and the minimum number of hours as the basic

---

acronym in Spanish) since the end of 2011, as it is registered in the report where the data is taken from. SISA can be accessed in the site https://sisa.msal.gov.ar/sisa.

44. The report dated in August 2020, has public access https://www.argentina.gob.ar/sites/default/files/informe_fdt_datos2019_vf-1.pdf.

45. World health statistics overview 2019: monitoring health for the SDGs, sustainable development goals. Geneva: World Health Organization; 2019. (WHO/DAD/2019.1). Licence: CC BY-NC-SA 3.0 IGO.

requirements. Moreover, it further explains that the exercise of these professions can 'jeopardize the public interest as well as the health'. When it comes to graduate and postgraduate health courses in Argentina, most courses are free and offered in the public sector for both locals and foreigners living in the country.

II. Medical Specialists

102. In Argentina, residences are essential for the formation of specialists at a post graduate level. Graduate residents can access it via public offer. With this system, young doctors can, on the one hand, deepen their prior knowledge and, on the other hand, gain experience in the job market. In this way, the residences become an attractive intensive training system for new graduates and new professionals. In Argentina, medical residencies were introduced by Dr Tiburcio Padilla, who created the first local residency in Clinical Semiology and Propaedeutics at the University of Buenos Aires.[46] Padilla was a regular teacher in that subject and introduced this model which was already prevalent in the United States of America (USA).

103. In Argentina, the system of residences was consolidated in the 1970s improving the quality and the coverage of assistance. It is yet important to highlight that already in 1960, The Public Health Secretary of State had adopted Resolution 1778 that defined the residence as 'a professional education system for graduates of medical schools, with training in full-time service, for a fixed term to prepare them for the integral, scientific, technical and social practice of one specialty'.

104. In the 1990s there was a significant increase in the number of private sector-associated housing, which started to become the valid way to access the certificate of the specialty. Ten days later, in the year 2000, the Ministry of National Health promoted an increase in national residence places. It is at this point that an important aspect was defined: the residency is not aimed at preparing the professional to be competent in the specific job but rather aims at refining the methodological skills of the resident so that they become more capable of working effectively in various contexts. In short, the residency is aimed at the better integration of the professional in the working environment of his specialty.

46. https://www.argentina.gob.ar/sites/default/files/tocoginecologia_0.pdf.

Chapter 2. The Practice of Medicine

105. Health professions in Argentina have been subject to constant regulation over the years, especially due to the relevance, responsibility and direct impact of the sector on the life and well-being of the population.

106. The legislative systems of the medical profession in Argentina aim to establish certain standards in professional regulation, ethical behaviour and training. In terms of the regulation of professional practice, two types should be distinguished: external regulation, set by the State itself; and self-regulation established by the profession itself through instruments such as codes of professional ethics. In Argentina, there are several entities authorized to issue professional licenses for different specialties. For example, in the city of Buenos Aires, the Ministry of Health is authorized to issue licenses for nursing, dentistry, pharmacy, biochemistry, nutrition and psychology. However, this is not the case in other provinces. In Greater Buenos Aires, it is the professional association authorized to license careers such as medicine or dentistry. Additionally, in counties such as Salta and Santa Fe, professional associations of each specialty are licensed.

107. Since 2001, the Register of the Federal Network of Health Professionals has been available in the Integral Health Information System of Argentina. There you can find all licensed professionals in every jurisdiction. In the national territory, the university degree is the enabling document to practice a particular specialty. However, there is a specialist diploma which is awarded by each province. The degree is relevant because it is a unique requirement to be part of the supplier lists and to be able to apply differentiated rates.

108. National Law 17132 – establishing the regulations for the practice of medicine, odontology, and all the activities in collaboration thereof – regulates the professional exercise in Buenos Aires city and in other provinces all around the country which have adhered to the norm which was passed and sanctioned on the 24th of January 1967. Law 23873, amending 17132, enumerates and specifies the necessary conditions to obtain the specialization certificate authorized by the Ministry of Health which is at the same time complemented by NEP Decrees 10/2003 and 587/2004.

109. Regarding the inclusion of new specialties, this means a multi-step process. First, the National Consultative Committee (composed of several professional, scientific and union bodies) is responsible for analyzing and presenting the proposal for registration of a new specialty. Then, the competent professional bodies carry out the technical analysis in order to forward the proposal to the Federal Health Council of Confederation of Employers in South Africa (COFESA). If the proposal is accepted, COFESA will have to take the necessary measures for its implementation.

110. Resolution 1105/2006 from the Ministry of Health created the Counselling Committee for the Practice for the Professions in health at a university level. Among other roles, this Committee oversees the specialization modalities validation and seeks common criteria and regulations of professions and specialization recognition at a federal level. It is aimed at eliminating asymmetries arising from several jurisdictions. The National Ministry of Health recognizes specialties for medicine, odontology, nursing, pharmacy, biochemistry and multi-professional specialties.

Chapter 3. Illegal Practice of Medicine

111. In Argentina, the illegal practice of medicine is typified in the National Criminal Code under section 208, establishing that The one who:

(1) without authorisation or degree, to use the art of cure or exceeding the limits of his/her authority announces, prescribes, administers, or habitually applies medications, waters, electricity, hypnotism, or any other means whatsoever with the aim of treating diseases in people, even it was for free;
(2) with degree or authorisation, to use the art of cure, announces, or promises the cure of illnesses in a fixed time or by secret or infallible means;
(3) with degree or authorisation to use the art of cure, gives his name to a third party not having a degree or authorization to perform the actions mentioned in subsection 1 of the section herein shall be sentenced to 15 days to one year imprisonment.

112. It is frequent to find the criminal type of section 208 associated with other criminal types such as for example section 247 of the same code, which establishes 'fifteen days to one year imprisonment for the one exercising acts of a certain profession which requires a special authorization, without having the corresponding degree or said authorization'. The very same section sets forth a fine for those who 'publicly carry a badge of a role or position they would not be performing, or arrogates themselves academic titles, professional degrees or honours not corresponding to them'.

113. Likewise, the forgery of documents in general (section 292 Penal Code) is also a crime that is usually connected to the actions seeking these illegal practices. The referred section reads:

> The one who either forges a document in total or in part or changes a true one, in such a way that can be harmful, shall be punished with six months to two years imprisonment, in the case it was a private instrument.
>
> If the forged or changed document were intended to prove a person's identity or the ownership or authorization to move in vehicles, the punishment will be three to eight years.
>
> For the purposes of the preceding paragraph, other documents to prove identity are those given to the members of the armed forces, the police, or the penitentiary, the identification cards, any and all types of identification documents, passports as well as certificates of delivery and certificates of birth issued by a competent authority.

114. The Argentinean Law goes further in this aspect and penalizes those who would use a forged or changed document or certificate, setting the same punishment as that of the perpetrator of the crime (section 296).

115. In the acts that constitute 'swindles and other types of frauds' (TITLE VI, Chapter IV of the Criminal Code), also to consider is section 172, that establishes 'one month to six years imprisonment for the one defrauding another with a false name, deceptive capacity, false titles, false pretence, abuse of trust, or pretending to have properties, credits, commission, company, or business or using any other scheme or ploy'

Chapter 4. Control over the Practice of Medicine

§1. Professional Liability

I. Civil Liability

A. Alleged Specialties Classifications

116. Several readings and interpretations have been made about the study of the civil responsibility in health in Argentina. A first interpretation, for example, makes a difference between the physicians on call from the rest of the physicians. The regulations for the physician on call – Minute nº 753 from the Physicians Association in Greater Buenos Aires, District III[47] – defines these professionals as those 'who carry out any and all tasks in the Emergency Room, whether temporarily or permanently, in a fixed or movable place belonging to Public or Private Medicine, Social Security System or of intermediary Entities' (section 1), being their role to 'consider the medical assistance of the patients admitted in hospital and the external demand as an urgent nature' with the obligation 'to perform the corresponding medical exam ensuring that the reason why a patient went to doctor or the sector of admittance so justifies it, without expressing tiredness due to his job in the working schedule' (section 6).

117. Nina Norma Noriega takes the words of Roberto Vázquez Ferreira to explain that 'the physician on call, as he undertakes a generic control and permanence obligation of the service, since the personnel is restrained for the necessary rest, will guarantee the service in the emerging cases during the course of his duty; specially in cases of emergency in which he will give the patient the first assistance reasonably or prudently begin required'.[48] The same author – Noriega – makes use of the criteria applied by the Civil and Commercial Chamber of Córdoba and concludes that 'the behaviour of the physician on call does not entail the cure or due care of the patient, but rather the likelihood of the patient being assisted or derived for the best possible treatment and the best advisable cure that enables his recovery. Thus, the on-call physician's main duty will be to prevent any and all circumstance that may put the patient's life at risk, ensuring the assistance to preserve his life.'

118. Likewise, Carolina Inés Musacchio highlights another point concerning the corresponding medical act, differentiating on the one hand 'the assistance medical act of necessity and healing', the typical act for which the real patient is treated; that is 'the voluntary medical act, or that of satisfaction', for those case in which the patient's health is not affected but for which he is seeking an improvement in his body, as in the case of the aesthetic surgeries or other such as the vasectomy.[49] The

47. https://www.colmed3.com.ar/imprimir/imprimir_legislacion_medico_de_guardia.html.
48. 'La responsabilidad del médico de guardia en el Código Civil y Comercial'; Noriega, Nina Norma; Ed. Rubinzal Culzoni, 'RC D 1120/2017'.
49. 'La responsabilidad civil de los médicos luego de la sanción del nuevo Código Civil y Comercial', Musacchio, Carolina Inés; Ed. Rubinzal Culzoni, 'RC D 1849/2016'.

same author recalls that the old Civil Code by Velez Sarsfield makes a distinction between the contractual and extra contractual responsibility which entails – among other things – different statutory time limits (ten years and two years respectively).

119. Last but not least, several authors point out that although the work of a professional doctor involves a general duty to give his best, that is, a professional doctor undertakes to transfer to the patient all the knowledge and skills that he possesses, he works diligently, but does not guarantee and does not provide a specific result, and in some cases, such as cosmetic surgery, there may be a commitment to the end result involved – a matter of particular interest to the end result. Furthermore, well-known lawmakers (among which we can mention Augusto Belluscio, Eduardo Zannoni and Atilio Alterini) have disregarded or minimized the existence or relevance of the debate between 'best efforts obligation' versus 'obligation on the end-results,'[50] since there exists plenty of studies and case laws intended to obliterate the limits between these two concepts.

120. An example regarding the aforementioned is the case entitled 'B., M. L. against Swiss Medical S.A. and others about Damages' (ruling of 19/06/2020), of the Room M of the National Civil Court which highlights that 'in the merely beautifying surgeries, the same as the rest of the cases, all of them refer to best efforts obligations. The key to a fair resolution of any case lies in the distribution of the burden of proof and the rigor with which it must be weighed. The proposed thesis has legal support. Consequently, according to law 17132, the doctor cannot guarantee a given result and a legal prohibition does not distinguish between cosmetic surgery and any other form (Articles 5 and 20). Therefore, if the promise is prohibited, it is inconsistent or contradictory to impose an obligation of result on the part of the doctor and to derive civil liability from its failure. Furthermore, cosmetic surgery has the same risk as the rest of the surgical procedures, as it is immersed in a very dangerous context. It is important to highlight those anaesthetics used (general or local, tissues are cut and several perilous instruments are used at the same time, etc. meaning that in plastic surgery, the same as in the rest of the medical services, the best-efforts obligation is implied. In any case, due to the special characteristics, the obligations assumed by the plastic surgeon should be tried with more severity,

---

50. In that vein, it is recommended to read 'La culpa y el distingo entre obligaciones de medio y de resultado' (Guilt and the distinction between best-effort obligation and obligation on end-results ilvolved), by Antonio Juan Rinessi (Revista de Derecho de Daños – La Culpa; year 2009, vol II; Publisher Rubizal Culzoni). The author realizes an eloquent and synthetic selection of quotes to expose that the rivalry between 'best-effort obligation' versus 'obligation on end-results involved' might entail a fruitless job, disproportionate and 'impoverishing' in legal terms. Rinessi takes Belluscio's example. 'The difference between best-effort obligation and obligation on end-results involved is non-existent since any and all obligation implies at the same time best-effort and results: it always tends to obtain a result or end, since it would otherwise lack purpose; and implies the presence of means tending to that end, without which it would also be impossible to conceive its essence. It would be utopic to separate the result from the best effort leading to that end. Thus, there would be no difference between both categories, not even ontological. This would be clear in the obligations to give and not to do; moreover, the same conclusion could be drawn in the obligations to give, that would always end-result involved.'

but without losing sight that any intervention, even the simplest one can entail unexpected consequences, impossible to foresee or prevent.'[51]

B. General Study

121. Apart from the different classifications to be taken into account and specific cases, according to the criteria already mentioned in the previous paragraph, the medical task implies an obligation of means. As Roberto A. Vazquez Ferreyra said, the fact that the doctor's obligation of means is unavoidable entails a subjective factor (fault), so his civil liability goes hand in hand. Without fault (including lato sensu and intention) there is no medical liability.[52] In this regard, the physician's task would not greatly differ from that of the liberal professionals and would have to be framed in each case's context pursuant to provisions under section 1724 of the Civil and Commercial Code of the Nation.

122. Said section, when referring to the subjective factors, establishes that: 'the subjective factors refer to those of attribution are guilt and intention. Guilt consists of the omission of the diligence due according to the nature of the people's obligation and circumstances, the space, and the time. It implies imprudence, negligence, and lack of knowledge in the job or profession. The criminal intent is configured by the harm intentionally produced or with an open indifference towards other's interests.' The greater the duty to act with prudence and full knowledge, the greater the diligence required by the agent and the greater the value of the predictability of the consequences. Likewise, where a special trust exists, the nature of the deed and the exceptional circumstances of the parties must also be taken into account. To evaluate certain behaviours, neither the particular condition nor the intellectual capacity of a particular person should be taken into account, except for contracts in which there is an exceptional degree of trust between the parties. In such cases, the degree of liability is estimated on the basis of the agent's extraordinary condition (section 1725).

123. Section 1726 provides further information about the liability, stating that 'harmful consequences which have link with the act causing the harm are reparable. Unless legally provided otherwise, immediate consequences and the foreseeable mediate one' (immediate consequences are those habitually taking place according to the ordinary and natural course of events and mediate consequences are those occurring only in connection with one single act and cannot be foreseen and that is why they are called 'casual consequences'. All this is elaborated in section 1727 of the Commercial and Civil Code).

---

51. Case '*B., M. L. v. Swiss Medical S.A. y otro s. Daños y perjuicios*', CNCiv. Sala M; 19/06/2020; Rubinzal Online; RC J 4767/20.
52. 'Responsabilidad del médico generalista', Vázquez Ferreyra, Roberto A.; Revista de Derecho de Daños, año 2003, Tomo III, Responsabilidad de los profesionales de la salud, Ed. Rubinzal Culzoni, 'RC D 1204/2012'.

124. The violation of the duty not to harm others or the failure to fulfil an obligation gives rise to compensation for the damage caused (section 1716). The claim for compensation for damage deriving from civil liability expires after three years (section 2561). Despite what has been elaborated so far, it is necessary to strengthen the predominant idea of the causal link between the harmful outcome and the behaviour of the healthcare professional. In other words, in the malpractice process, the application is accepted on condition that the professional's conduct was the real cause, for example, of death. If the event occurred, the fault would be irrelevant in the liability analysis; 'It is not enough that the event was, in the concrete case, the sine qua non for the harm;' – Musaccio defines – 'it is also necessary that, by virtue of the probability and foreseeability judgments in abstract, it entails a cause suitable for that end'.[53]

125. Law 26529 – on the rights of the patient in relation to his relations with health professionals and institutions – has an explicit and perhaps obvious principle in section 11bis when it states it 'no acting professional who has acted under the provisions of the present law, shall be subject to either civil, criminal, or administrative liability derived from the fulfilment thereof.' As a counterpart, the law establishes that 'notwithstanding the civil or criminal responsibility, failure to comply with the emerging responsibilities from this law from the part of the professionals and the authorities in charge of the health institutions shall be deemed as a serious offense, subject to the national jurisdiction of the penalties set forth under title VIII of the Law 17132 – Legal Regulations of the Practice of Medicine, Odontology and Auxiliary Activities thereof and, in the local jurisdiction they shall be subject to the penalties corresponding to legal regulations of medicine in force in those jurisdictions', under section 21.

126. This ordinance specifies the responsibility in certain aspects, for example with regard to confidentiality in the doctor-patient relationship (*see* 'Data protection', Chapter 1; part II), which is not only subject to the specialized personnel treating, but also to the supreme authority of the health establishment, as well as to social security bodies and any other public or private entity that accesses it. It is important to note that the signature of the informed consent form by the patient should not be considered as a license in favour of the doctor, since the professionals remain responsible for certain acts.

II. Criminal Liability

A. General Framework of the Criminal Liability

127. The nation's penal code on many occasions refers to offenses that may be included in the activities of healthcare professionals. In general, it is possible to distinguish intentional crimes – such as those in which knowledge and will are present in the criminal typology, such as homicide – from culpable crimes – characterized

53. *Ibid.* nº 56.

by imprudent, negligent or faulty fulfilment of duty. At first, it is good to consider that guilt generates responsibility and that the criminal action belongs to those who are naturally competent. Criminal liability, in turn, is personal (non-transferable and directed against a human being); it is therefore not possible to blame a legal person, institution or partnership.

128. Additionally, it is understood that the physicians working for public institutions are considered public servants which entails a great liability.[54] Section 77 of the Criminal Code defines 'public servant' and 'public employee' as 'the one temporarily or permanently holding a position either by popular election or appointment by a competent authority.' In Argentina, civil servants have a general obligation to report offences: Article 177 of the Code of Criminal Procedure states that this obligation includes 'crimes prosecutable by operation of law' in the case of public servants that know them in the course of their duties; and in the case of 'physicians, nurses, pharmacists and others practising any branch on the art of cure, regarding crimes against life, and physical integrity they know about when rendering assistance in their profession, unless the known act were under the professional secret.'

129. In the same vein, the non-compliance of the duties of a public servant as well as the cover-up of illegal acts have grievous consequences for the perpetrators. The law establishes that 'the public servant who adopts regulations or resolutions against the constitutions or national or provincial laws, or executes the existing law or regulations of this kind or else does not execute the ones he is obliged, shall be punished with one month to two years imprisonment and special disqualification for double time' (section 248 Criminal Code) and the one 'who does not report the commission of the crime or the perpetrators or accomplices of the crime when he is liable to pursue the criminal prosecution of a crime of this kind', shall be punished with six months to three years imprisonment, after a third party has committed a crime without him even participating. The prescription is suspended in case of crimes committed in the exercise of the public role, for those committing them, as long as any of them is in a public position. (Section 67 Criminal Code).

130. Moreover, we can find other regulations which can reach the health profession even when they do not specifically mention it. In the case of section 84 of the Criminal Code, it provides that 'the one who out of due to negligence, imprudence, lack of expertise in his craft or profession, or due to non-observance of the laws and of his duties causes the death of an individual shall be punished with one (1) to fine (5) years imprisonment and special disqualification, if applicable, with five (5) to ten (10) years. The minimum punishment will be two (2) years in the case of more than one fatal victim'.

131. The criminal code contains a whole chapter on the abandonment of persons (sections 106 to 108), a concept closely related to the professionals' and health

54. The case law and studies have considered this wording, for example, in the case entitled 'C. P. D. E. about limitation and costs', decision of the VI of the Chamber of Crime.

teams' performance (especially when failing to provide medical intervention or when causing death by failure to aid in due course). Section 106 clearly establishes that 'the one putting other person's life in danger, whether that being in helplessness, abandoning the person who is unable to fend for himself, and that he should be taking care of or that he himself has handicapped, shall be punished with two to six years imprisonment. The punishment shall be three to ten years imprisonment or reclusion, if as a consequence of the abandonment, there was serious harm to the victim's body or health. In case of death, the punishment shall be five to fifteen years imprisonment.'

132. Moreover, section 108 provides monetary penalties for 'the one who finds a lost or helpless child under 10 years of age, or a wounded, invalid or threatened person of any danger and fails to render assistance without detriment to himself, or to immediately give notice to the authority.'

133. The job of health professionals implies dealing with hazardous situations and results that without being expected, do not deserve to be blameworthy. Thus, it is obvious that section 34 of the Criminal Code, when referring to competence, sets forth that shall not be punishable, those under the assumption that, 'they caused a harm so as to avoid a greater harm they did not know about' (subsection 3) or 'if they were acting in the call of duty or in the legitimate exercise of their right, authority or position' (subsection 4°), both subsections are naturally applied to physicians.

B. Action Resulting in Several Criminal Offenses

134. The illegal practice of medicine generally entails several criminal offences. Argentinean law provides that 'when a crime is subject to more than one criminal sanction, the highest one shall be applied' (section 54 of the Criminal Code of the Nation). In addition, Article 55 of the same code specifies that when several independent offenses have been committed and are liable to the same type of penalty, the penalty applicable to the offender must have at least, at the highest minimum and at the most, the sum of the individual offenses corresponding to the maximum penalties. However, this sum cannot exceed fifty years of imprisonment.

135. In the case of several independent criminal offenses punished with divisible imprisonment penalties-according to section 56 of the Criminal Code – 'the most serious penalty shall be applied, considering the crimes of the lowest penalty. If any of the penalties were not divisible, this only one will only be applied, unless in the case of life imprisonment and temporary reclusion in which case life imprisonment will be applied. The disqualification and the fine shall always be applied, without subject to the provisions in the first paragraph.' (Section 56). Concerning the presiding section, the relative seriousness of the penalties of different kinds shall be set by the order in which they are enumerated in section 5[55] of the Criminal Code (section 57).

55. The referred s. 5 sets forth that 'The sanctions this Code established are namely: incarceration, prison, fine and disqualification.'

136. So as to conclude this argument concerning multiple criminal offenses, the Criminal Code sets forth under section 58 that 'the aforementioned rules shall be applied also in the case that after a prosecution has been issued with the final ruling, the same person is to be tried for another crime; or in the case of two or more final rulings due to infringement of said rules. The judge who has decided on the highest punishment, at the party's request, shall pronounce a unique sentence, without changing the statements of the facts contained in the others. Whenever, due to any reason whatsoever, the federal justice in case of its jurisdiction, cannot apply this rule, the ordinary national or provincial justices knowing about the criminal fine shall intervene accordingly.'

III. Vicarious Liability

137. The activity of the health professional is also subject to the provisions of the Civil and Commercial Code relating to the liability of the employer for the act of the employee. Article 1753 of the Nation's Civil and Commercial Code states: 'The employer is vicariously liable for damages caused by his employees if the damages occur in the performance of recommended duties. The ignorance of the employee does not exempt the employer. The liability of the employer is linked to that of the employee at the same time. Thus, "when the harm suffered by the patients is the result of the physician's job, the clinic or hospital has to indirectly respond". This last quote corresponds to the ruling "P. C. U. *v.* Sanatorio Posadas S.A. and other about damages", from the Federal Court of Appeals from Posadas (dated on 17/03/2021), though the decision is founded under section 1113 from the already derogated Civil Code, the new code shares the same view. The sanatory – as the ruling illustrates "A., O. E. and other about Obra Social of El Gráfico staff and others about medical Liability", decision from the National Federal Civil and Commercial Chamber, Room III, dated 16 June 2020 shall dispose the necessary resources so that the employees – physicians and the hospital staff – can render the required services and assistance. Not only do they have to respond for the physician's liability, but also for the defects of the things – all far from the physician's job – provided that they put the patient's life or health at risk.' In the case of the clinic, 'the attribution factor is objective, since once the guilt of the physician's is proved, the sanatorium shall respond based on tacit obligation of security (CNCiv. Room D, proceedings "G., M.F. and others against Centro Médico Lacroze and others" dated on 28/3/96, LL 1996-D-450; López Herrera, Edgardo, Teoría general de la responsabilidad civil, Buenos Aires, Lexis Nexis, page 590 and the following.)', which is different from the factor of subjective attribution that is upon the physician as already elaborated on in the Civil Liability item.

138. This means that in some cases the doctor and the health institutions may be jointly and severally liable to the health insurer or the union insurer. Even if hygienic medical care is not provided, the health insurance company or union-administered health insurer may be held liable even if the doctor or clinic fails to provide the care. This is what happened in the case 'A., O. E. and others against Obra Social of the El Gráfico staff and others about medical liability'. In that case, the Court of Appeals just made the union-run medical insurance responsible, 'for the clinic's failure to assist, the objective legal imputation of the delay in the medical assistance of the member arises from the weighing of the evidence submitted, without the physicians or the rest of the staff having to be held responsible'. The sanatorium under analysis was a supplier of union-run medical insurance. The lack of organization of the emergency room staff caused a one-and-a-half-hour delay between the diagnosis and the Caesarea: ' … this was, in turn, the cause of the harm (birth of a dead baby due to intrauterine foetal anoxia).'

139. The same occurs, for example, in the case of intrahospital infections, that 'as a recoverable damage, it presents a great challenge in terms of evidence due to the difficulty to demonstrate when, how and where from the pathogenic microorganism was introduced into the body. In this case, first and foremost, the services offered by clinics, sanatoriums and medical assistance companies in general must be rendered in such a way that in normal and foreseeable conditions of use, shall not run a risk whatsoever for the health or physical integrity of the patients being treated by them (section 42, National Constitution Nacional; section 5, Law 24240). Basically, it is the medical companies' objective responsibility, although they shall not be held liable if there is categorical evidence of an endogenous infection since such a factor configure the evidence of the cause as external and that breaks the causal relationship. Furthermore, it is worth saying that if there was a doubt for the omission of not having the necessary documentation, the consequences are not to be assumed by the victim, but rather by the ones who were in better conditions to provide them.' (Proceeding of the case entitled 'Noilhan, Víctor Hugo against Swiss Medical Aseguradora de Riesgos del Trabajo about Damages', decision of the National Civil Courts of Appeals, Room M, dated 10/09/2021).

140. Finally, a recurring actor in this type of process should be mentioned: insurance companies which are usually hired by doctors, clinics or sanatoriums and health insurance companies managed by trade unions. The activity of insurance companies is regulated by Law 17418 (Insurance Contract). 'The insurance agent shall serve their judicial sentence in the procedural terms', under section 116 of said law, a section widely applied in the studies and case law regarding the matter; the same as the provisions under section 118 since 'the judgment to be pronounced shall be res judicata concerning the insurance agent and shall be enforceable in so far as the insurance in concerned. In this trial, or in the execution of judgment, the insurance broker will not be able to file pleas produced after the event'. The insurer will not be released if the insured acknowledges, during the investigation, the actions deriving from his responsibility. The Insured must report the event from which his liability derives within a period of three days from the event, provided he is or is aware of it; or from the claim of a third party if he was not previously aware of it. He notifies the insurer without delay when the third party files objections. (Section 115).

§2. Quality Assurance

141. Aside from the responsibilities of the Superintendence of Health Services – as it was mentioned in II.b.iii., such as to control and supervise the Health Services to ensure the compliance of the policies in the area; to oversee the operation of the Union-run insurance companies of the Health Insurance Agents, the intervening suppliers, and any and all other health institutions providing health services; and to control the compliance of the ethical obligations corresponding to the Entity and all its dependencies; and to develop control mechanisms and processes against fraud and corruption, Argentina has had the National Program of Quality Assurance of Medical Assistance (PNGCAM) improved by Decree 1424/97 since 1992.

142. The latter established that the mentioned Program should be legally binding in all the national health institutions, in the National System of Health Insurance, in union-run insurance companies and in the National Institute of Social Services for Pensioners (also known by its acronym INSSJP or as PAMI: the biggest union-run insurance company in Latin America, covering approximately 5 million pensioners and their families and war veterans), among other institutions.

143. The purpose of this program has been from the beginning 'to regulate the activities related to the sanitary system- so as to ensure the quality in the services rendered to the population- and to propose measures necessary to guaranty the quality thereof', as it is set forth under section 2 of the Decree 1424/97, based on nine basic tasks:

(a) Risk-criteria classification and authorization according to the category of the health institution.
(b) Health team members' certification and re-certification.
(c) Establishment of organization and management standards and manuals of procedures concerning Health Services.
(d) Establishment of diagnosis and therapeutic algorithms regarding the most frequent sanitary problems based on specificity, sensitivity, and cost-benefit criteria.
(e) Establishment of production and performance standards concerning Health Services.
(f) Technical cooperation and advice to the jurisdictions, hospital and the entities helping design regulations and other aspects related to the development and implementation of the Program.
(g) Establishment of control and inspection regulations for the fulfilment of the Program.
(h) Quality assessment of the institutions rendering health services and the certification of such institutions.
(i) Results-impact analysis and the user's satisfaction rate.

144. Decree 178/2017 introduced subtle variations to this scheme whereas Resolution 856-E/2017 updated the conceptual axes of the program, adapting them to the current times in a matter whose development and growth require periodic adjustments.

§3. Review Boards

145. The fragmentation of the Argentine health system is also reflected in the various advisory bodies from the area concerned.

146. For example, to obtain the single certificate of disability – proof of identity of a person with a specific disability – the Ministry of Health must set up a medical commission to assess this condition. This panel must be installed by specialized professionals, as stipulated in Article 3 of National Decree 498/83 (defining the provisions of Law 22431 on the integral protection system for people with disabilities). This medical board has nothing to do with the medical examination or the interdisciplinary team that belongs to the prepaid drugs or union insurance companies set up to evaluate the services, drugs and supplies they provide. Act 24901, under section 11, established that 'people with disabilities who are members of union-run insurance companies, shall have access through the latter, by means of interdisciplinary teams to that effect, to individual, family and group evaluations and orientation, communal promotional-preventive programs, and to any and all actions tending to favour the social integration and insertion of the people with a disability in the basic health system.' This interdisciplinary team sets guidelines for the duration during which a disabled person can have access to a given service and, in turn, when there are clear signs of stagnation in their general condition, must advise users on other services according to their current possibilities, from a therapeutic, educational and re-educational point of view and are in a chronic state.

§4. Disciplinary Organisations

I. Order of Physicians

147. In addition to professional associations, there are several organizations in Argentina that bring together health professionals. One of the oldest is the Argentine Medical Association (AMA), founded in 1891 but with legal capacity since 1914, today with a total of thirty-seven thousand members, forty-three AMAs, seven associations and twenty-five active committees in various delegations throughout the country.[56] Several Professional Academies complete the plural and federal scheme, and other associations all around the globe such Austrian-Argentinean Medical Association, the Rioplatense Association of Internal Medicine, the Japanese-Argentinean Association, the Chilean-Argentinean Medical Association, and the French-Argentinean Medical Association which have their central office in

56. https://www.ama-med.org.ar/page/Institucional-Historia.

the AMA Argentinean Medical Association. This clearly shows that the Argentinean Medical community´s endeavour is to adopt criteria and principles towards jointly progress.

148. AMA itself envisions ‘to offer the health professionals the most comprehensive program of activities ensuring the ongoing scientific development by means of the most modern technologies and the widest coverage of communication in our programs’. To meet such an objective, the association has a medical journal and an Editorial Department whose first publication was in 1892. It also has a physical library and, since 1995, also a digital medical library. The Graduate School is also a cornerstone in the continuing education that the institution seeks for its members and provides training in various subjects for both local and foreign physicians.

II. Professional Codes

149. The AMA has drafted a Code of Ethics for the Health Team, a tool that has been expanded and refined over the past twenty years, has three editions and with which the Argentine Association of Medical Ethics has collaborated, among other prestigious institutions. Its last edition, in 2016, was marked by a secular spirit in the exercise of the profession, without losing sight of the idea ‘health is everyone’s responsibility’, concept that has been repeated once and again in the Code, without that overshadowing the health professionals’ conduct and responsibility.

150. The introduction of the first edition of this Code ‘in the context of the Ethics and Professional Ethics, establishes the duties and commitments and exemptions, the scope of the responsibility and actions of the health professionals. In the same vein, are the parameters by means of which their behaviours are examined, approved, or disapproved, extoled, or condemned by their peers in the association or by the society in general. When someone strays from the norm, it can be for variations or deviation from the established behaviour.’[57] Since the first edition, the need to understand health in teams and the need to pay particular attention to professionals due to the information provided by the media is very clear. The second edition deals with technological progress and new behaviours introduced by a constantly evolving society, the digital divide, assisted reproduction – ‘designer babies’ were mentioned there- and the global challenges in the field of the health.

151. The Argentinean Medical Association is not the only institution that has developed a Code of Ethics oriented to outline guidelines concerning health professionals’ behaviour. The Medical Confederation of Argentina, also known as COMRA (medical-union institution that fights for the labour rights of professionals all around the country and the exercise of the right to health) also created a Code of

57. https://www.ama-med.org.ar/images/uploads/files/CODIGO%20DE%20ETICA%203ra%20Edici%C3%B3n.pdf.

Ethics[58] that from its first publication in the year 1995 has been periodically updated. The latest version has been enriched by the work of the Ethics Committee of the Medical Association of the City of Buenos Aires – FEMECA – as well as by the comparative analysis with other codes of ethics in the world. The latest version of this code included studies on information systems, the role of the physician in assisted reproduction, dignity to be considered at the beginning and end of life, organ donation and transplantation, among others.

152. Clinical history, research and human experimentation, scientific and union relations with other institutions, quality of medical care, notification of medical advertising, incompatibilities, rights and fees of doctors are just some of the topics covered in the text grafted by COMRA, which is consistent with Advances and debates in the academic context and across medical practice are constantly evolving.

III. Biomedical Ethics Committee

153. In Argentina, the development of Biomedical ethics committee -in the public as well as the private sector- begins in the 80, in the Clinics Hospital in Buenos Aires (1984), the neonatal service in the Italian Hospital in Buenos Aires (1984) and the Oncology Centre of Excellence of the Mainetti Foundation (1987).[59]

154. Law 24742, of the year 1996, established the obligation that every hospital in the public health and security system should have an Ethics Hospital Committee which should have a role of counselling, study, training, and supervision in the investigation concerning the ethical issues arising from the hospital medicine practice. The same rule states that hospital ethics committees operate as interdisciplinary teams of doctors, paramedics, lawyers, philosophers, and human behavioural science professionals, who may or may not be hospital staff. They will carry out their tasks under the direction of the hospital and will be outside the hierarchical structure.

155. Among the issues to be dealt with by the Hospital Ethics Committees, there are:

(a) Reproductive Technologies.
(b) Eugenics.
(c) Experimenting in humans.
(d) Artificial prolongation of life.
(e) Euthanasia.
(f) Patient-physician relationship.
(g) The value and quality of life.

58. https://comra.org.ar/codigo-etica/.
59. 'Comités de bioética'; Maglio; Ignacio; DELS article avaible at https://salud.gob.ar/dels/entradas/comites-de-bioetica.

(h) Health assistance.
(i) Genetics.
(j) Organ's transplant.
(k) Mental health.
(l) Patients' rights.
(m) Professional Secret.
(n) Rational use of resources.

156. The Committee's opinion has no binding force and 'shall exempt neither the intervening professional nor the hospital authorities from ethical or legal responsibility' (section 4, Law 24742).

157. In the provincial jurisdiction, the regulations concerning the bioethics committees are also relevant. For instance, the Province of Buenos Aires has Law 11044, which under section 7 establishes that 'all research about human beings shall be immediately discontinued, whenever the researcher from the Research Committee of the Health Institution in charge of it, notices some risks and/or damages derived from it which can affect one or more participants. Moreover, this shall apply when one or more of the subjects under study so requires.' Likewise, the researcher in charge, the Ethics Committee, the Institution in charge or the Ministry of Health shall cancel or discontinue the research in the case of any adverse effect whether that is ethical or technical. (Section 25).

158. Section 36 of the provincial law is the one that sets forth that 'in every Health Institution in which research is conducted, an Ethics Committee and Research Committee shall constantly operate in accordance with what is established in the law. The Ethics Committee shall be integrated by, at least, a professional member qualified in research not belonging to the institution, by professional members qualified in health research, by laymen capable of representing the moral, cultural, and social values of the groups of people participating in the research, and apt for reasonably knowing the risks and benefits of the research, as well as by other lawyers and/or interdisciplinary professionals with qualifications in accordance with the nature of the research.'

159. Buenos Aires city also has a law concerning the creation and regulation of Bioethics Committees in the health system of the capital (Law 3302). This law defines ethics as 'a discipline whose main objective is the systematic study of the human behaviour in the context of the science of life and health analysed from the perspective of the dilemma and the ethical debate generated in the society' and instructs that 'the Bioethics committees are interdisciplinary, intersectoral, and interinstitutional entities whose overriding objective is counselling and teaching about hospital issues.'

160. Among the roles of the Committees under CABA law, there are:

(1) Foster the training and formation of the hospital personnel.
(2) Counsel about ethical issue in the relationships regarding the life, the death, the health, the illness, the medical practice, and the social problems related to the health and to give advice to the different institutions created for the Constitution and the laws concerning the bioethics issues. The decisions will be made in relation to the time each case requires.
(3) Consider and apply the principle of rationality in the use of the resources available.
(4) Respect the professional secret and in all the issues under analysis.
(5) Foster respect for human dignity.
(6) Promote the ongoing formation and training of the Hospital Bioethics Committee members.
(7) Develop their activities interrelated with the other Hospital Bioethics Committees.

161. These committees are integrated into an ad-honorary board of directors of 10 to 15 members who, among other things, cannot belong to the structure of the hospital. The same law creates the Ministerial Ethics Committee within the framework of the Ministry of Health, whose main role is to serve as an advisory framework for the Bioethics Committees. The ministerial bioethics committee is the one that creates the guidelines that bioethics committees must follow when developing and drafting their own rules of procedure.

162. In relation to bioethics, other regulations are important at a national level such as Decree 426/1998 (National Committee on Biomedical Ethics); Resolution 1678/2007 (List of clinical trials in human beings); Resolution 1002/2016 (National Advisory Committee on Research Ethics) Resolution 2026-E/2016 about Development and operation of the latter committee and Provision 1474-E/2017 establishing the Rules of Procedures of this entity; and Resolution 1727/2018 (Ethics Committee for the Health Research Bureau). Cases in point in each province: Buenos Aires has Resolution 4107/2009 about the Central Ethics Committee, while Córdoba has Law 9011 about Cordoba Bioethics Counsel; in Corrientes, there is Law 5896 which provides instructions about the Hospital Ethics Committees; in Misiones, Law 4334 has the same role as the Law in Corrientes; in San Luis Decree 5495/2006 forms the Provincial Bioethics Committee, among other local instruments composing the regulations in each province.

Part II. Physician-Patient Relationship

Chapter 1. General Description

§1. Rights and Duties of Physicians and Patients

163. Law 26529 – of the rights of the Patient in their relationship with the Physician and the Healthcare Institutions-, in force since the year 2010, sets forth the interaction between the users of the system and the specialists and in the institutions in Argentina, as indicated by the name of the law. This legal body basically contains the patients' rights and the professionals and institutions' obligations, with a clear protectionist view towards those requiring medical services since they are the most vulnerable part of the system and of the relationship itself.

164. Proof of this protective nature is section 2 of such law, which contains seven basic rights in the relationship between the patient and the healthcare professionals, the healthcare providers and any other third party involved:

(a) *Assistance*. The patient, especially children and adolescents, has the right to be assisted by health professionals, without prejudice or any discrimination based on their ideas or beliefs, political, religious, socioeconomic conditions, race, gender, sexual orientation or any other condition. The operating healthcare professional can only be exempted from the obligation to care if another competent healthcare professional has taken charge of the patient.
(b) *Respectful and dignified treatment*. The patient and his relatives and companions have the right to be treated with dignity by the intervening agents of the system with regard to his personal and moral convictions, mainly in relation to his socio-cultural condition, his sex, his shyness and his intimacy, whatever regardless of the patient's situation and suffering of the patient might be.
(c) *Intimacy*. Any and all medical-assistance related activity tending to obtain, classify, utilize, administer, keep, and transmit clinic information and documentation of the patients' must observe the strict respect for the human dignity, the independent will as well as the due care of the intimacy and confidentiality of the sensible date, notwithstanding the provisions under Law n° 25326 (about Protection of personal data).
(d) *Confidentiality*. The patient is entitled to the due non-disclosure from the part of the any and all persons participating in the drafting or elaboration of the clinical

documentation or having access to the content thereof, unless otherwise expressly stated by the competent judicial authority or authorized by the very same patient.

(e) *Independent will.* The patient is entitled to accept or reject certain medical or biological therapies or procedures, with or without stating the reason thereof, as well as to further reverse his independent will. Children and teenagers have the right to intervene in the terms under Law Nº 26061 (about Integral Protection of the Children and Teenagers) so as to make decisions about medical or biological procedures compromising their health or life.

(f) *Sanitary information.* The patient is entitled to receive the necessary sanitary information concerning his health. The right to sanitary information includes the right to not receive such information. As regards this, we find here one of the few duties in the regulation of Law 26529 (Decree 1089/2012) imposed to the patients: that of – if this is the case – expressing their will to exercise the right of not receiving the sanitary information in relation to their health, tests, or treatments by means of a consent in writing, which will be recorded in their clinic history. In such a case, the patient must inform who is authorized to receive such information and to decide about the treatment, or, in its case, give authorization so that the corresponding decisions can be made by themselves or the professionals treating the condition, in compliance with sections 4 and 6 of the law N° 26529, amended by law n° 26742 and the provisions of Decree 1089/2012.

(g) *Medical Inter-consultation.* The patient is entitled to receive the sanitary information in writing to obtain a second medical opinion about the diagnosis, forecast or treatment related to their condition.

165. The flip side of these basic rights – as it has already been stated – lies in the obligations of the physicians. Hence, the specialists and the healthcare organization are responsible for the assistance; the obligation to observe 'the strict respect for the human dignity and the independent will'; the duty to respect the patient's decision or that of their legal representative in case the former accepts or rejects a medical treatment, as well as the duty to accept the specific directives fixed by the patient. The institutions must keep a record of the patient's medical information, as at their request, they shall have the obligation to supply a copy thereof, always keeping in mind that the patient is the sole owner of the clinical history, among other duties established under the norm.

§2. Informed Consent

166. Law 25629 dedicates a complete chapter to informed consent, which is defined as, under section 5, the statement of sufficient will performed by the patient, or by their legal representatives in its case, issued after receiving from the intervening physician clear, precise, and suitable information regarding:

(a) their condition;
(b) the suggested procedure, with clear specificity of the objectives sought;

(c) the expected benefits of the procedure;
(d) the foreseeable risks, pain, and side effects;
(e) The reference to alternative procedures and the risks, benefits, and prejudices regarding the suggested procedure;
(f) The foreseeable consequences of the non-realization of the proposed procedure or the alternatives thereof.

167. Customarily, all professional acts in the medical sanitary field require the patient's prior written consent, whether that is a private or public institution. Even though this consent is in essence verbally informed, there can be exceptions that must be necessary in writing: in the case of admissions, surgery, invasive therapeutic and diagnosis treatments; procedures with risk implications according to the Patient's Rights Law (this regulation includes, among other events, the research of therapeutic and preventive methods with human beings); and the revocation of the written informed consent, which must be specified in the same instrument in which it was given, together with the detail of the consequences the patient expressly declares he is aware of, duly undersigned by him and with the intervention of the acting professional. This further means that informed consent can be rebuked, and the acting professional must respect that decision and clearly state that in the clinical history.

168. Finally, it is worth mentioning the cases of exception in which the acting professional is exempted from requiring informed consent. Such cases – construed in a restrictive fashion – are provided in section 9 of Law 25629 and are only two. This first is if the public health would be in great danger which must be declared by the corresponding Sanitary Authority; thus, in such context, 'the refusal to a treatment may entail the loss of benefits or rights or else to the coercive imposition of some treatments, pursuant to the legislation in force' as clearly set forth in this section. The second case is in the event of an emergency with great danger for the health or life of the patient and the latter was not able to give his own consent or by means of a legal representative. These exceptions must be stated in the clinical history with the specific reasons by which informed consent cannot be given as well as the practices and measures taken without it.

§3. Privacy

169. The right to intimacy – listed as one of the fundamental ones of any patient – implies that any medical-assistance activity tending to obtain, classify, utilize, administer, keep and transmit clinical information or documentation of the patient must observe respect for the human dignity and the independent will, as well as the due respect for intimacy and the confidentiality of the sensitive data which reveals the ethnic origin, political opinions, religious, philosophical or moral convictions, union memberships and information about the health or sexual life. This duty is closely related to the confidentiality the healthcare professionals and the institutions must respect regarding the patient.

§4. Secrecy

170. Confidentiality, as it was previously mentioned, is a fundamental right of the patient and it is the professionals' and the institutions' basic role to preserve it. Thus, it is the patient's right that any and all persons participating in the elaboration or manipulation of the clinical documentation, or having access to the content, should keep it confidential unless otherwise provided by the competent judicial authority or authorized by the patient himself.

171. In short, section 2 subsection 'd' of Law 26529 establishes that a patient is entitled to the non-disclosure of the clinical documentation in the hands of the healthcare professionals or their collaborators without his expressed authorization, with exceptions or otherwise judicially provided and to prevent greater damage due to public health. All these cases in which the confidential data is disclosed shall be duly registered in the clinical history and informed to the patient unless otherwise judicially provided. The duty of confidentiality is extended to all persons accessing the clinical documentation, even to those acting as services providers or financers.

§5. Complaints

172. Notwithstanding the corresponding criminal or civil liability, the non-compliances of the obligations emerging from Law 26529 on the part of the professionals and institutions responsible for the assistance, shall constitute a serious fault, being liable for prosecution in the national jurisdiction of the sanctions provided for in Title VIII of Law 17132 – Legal Regime of the Exercise of Medicine, Odontology and Auxiliary Activities thereof; and, in the local jurisdictions, liable for similar prosecution pursuant to the legal regime of the exercise of medicine in force in every jurisdiction.

173. The cited Title VIII of Law 17132 sets forth as part of the sanctions, the license suspension of the non-compliant professionals or the authorization suspension of the institution incurring in the sanctions of said law, warnings and total or partial closure of the consulting rooms, clinics, laboratories, and other institutions committing a crime subject to sanctions.

174. In the case of violation of the duty of confidentiality, the Law of the Patient's Rights applies not only to the acting profession but also to the institution's maximum authority and those of the social security agencies or of any other public or private institution having access to it.

§6. Access to Medical Records

175. Chapter IV of Law 26529 is reserved for the medical records that are 'the complete obligatory chronological paged account containing all tests and actions performed to the patient by healthcare professionals and paramedics', the way section 12 of such regulation so describes it. The patient is the owner of the medical records and so upon his mere request, he must be provided with them within forty-eight hours, except in the case of an emergency. These medical records must be given to the requesting party and authenticated by a competent authority of the healthcare institution. The medical records may be contained in magnetic support as long as the necessary means are furnished towards the integrity, authenticity, immutability, durability, and recoverability of the data contained therein timely and in due form.

176. The medical records are covered with a veil of inviolability meaning that healthcare public as well as private providers and the professionals – owners of consulting rooms – oversee the safekeeping thereof and must furnish the necessary means to avoid access to the information contained therein by unauthorized people. This obligation shall be in force for the term of ten years from the latest registration in the medical records.

177. The legitimate individuals to require medical records represent a *numerus clausus*. The first natural legitimate party is the patient himself and his legal representative. The second is his/her spouse or the person living with him in civil partnership. This same subsection of section 19 refers to the forced heirs 'in that case, with the patient's authorization, except when he is unable to grant it'. Finally, physicians and other healthcare professionals are granted this power whenever they have the patient's or their legal representative's expressed authorization. Healthcare professionals shall have access to the medical records in the case of: (a) being the acting professional; (b) the public health or other people's health or life was in danger due to the reasons stated by the sanitary authority; (c) being it necessary the access to the information for the realization of medical audits or for the job of the healthcare providers on condition that the necessary means be furnished to preserve the confidentiality of the data inherent to the patient.

178. In the case of refusal to access the medical records or even the delay or silence from the part of the responsible in charge of the safekeeping of such instruments, the legitimated individuals may file a 'habeas data' petition to ensure access to and obtention thereof and the most suitable and fastest procedure shall apply in the context of each jurisdiction. In the national jurisdiction, that shall be free of charge.

Chapter 2. The Physician-Patient Relationship

§1. The Minor Patient

179. Section 2 of Law 26529 – of the Patients' Rights in relation to the Healthcare Professionals and Institutions – makes a special point concerning underaged patients and their physicians. Hence, among the users' rights, there are 'first kids and teenagers' to 'be assisted by the healthcare professionals, without any distinction or undermining whatsoever due to their ideas, religious or political views, socio-economic situation, race, sexual orientation or any other reasons'. The acting healthcare professional can only be exempted from the duty to assist when another competent professional has effectively assumed the responsibility.

180. The very same section of this law, when dealing with the users' independent will, clearly establishes that 'the patient is entitled to accept or refuse certain medical or biological procedures or therapies, with or without expressing a reason, as well to further revoke their statement of will' and that 'the children and teenagers are entitled to intervene in the terms of Law Nº 26061 concerning the decision-making about biological or medical procedures and therapies involving their health or life'.

181. Law 26061 aforementioned is the Integral Protection for Children and Teenagers Act, which also establishes clear guidelines about treatments the population deserves in the context of medical institutions. Some cases in point, it is established that every healthcare institution shall primarily assist children, teenagers, and pregnant women, those who are entitled to 'receive integral health assistance, the necessary medical assistance and equal access to the healthcare services and actions of prevention, promotion, information, protection, early diagnosis, duly treatment and recovery of health' (section 14, subsection d).

182. In Argentina, an underaged individual is one who has not turned 18 years of age, whereas the teenager – a new incorporation of the Civil and Commercial Code in force as from August 2015 – is one that has turned 13 years of age, as it is defined under section 25 of the Civil and Commercial Code of Nation. This very same legislation establishes references concerning the exercise of the rights of the underaged. As a general rule, the underaged exercise their right by means of their legal representatives; in any case, the underaged having the necessary maturity can exercise the rights they are allowed to under the legislation in force.

183. However there exist exceptions to the rule: for instance, the underaged have the right to be heard in any trial or decision they are affected by – 'decisions about them', so establishes the legislation with prudence and discernment – conception that has been consolidated by the new substantive Code. Hence concerning the presumption for teens between 13 to 16 years of age, they will be able to decide on their own in cases of non-invasive or non-life or physical integrity-threatening procedures.

184. This Code also establishes that in conflict of interests with their legal representatives, the underaged can intervene with legal counsel. In the case of teenagers, regarding invasive treatments risking their health or integrity or life, the teenager can give his consent with his parents' advice; the dispute is then settled considering the higher interest, based on the medical opinion about the consequences of the realization or not of the medical procedure. Finally, from 16 years of age, a teenager is considered an adult to make decisions regarding his own body care.

185. Judge María Victoria Fama makes a distinction in this section 26 of the Code, namely 'a compound system built up as from two variables: one subjective related to mobile age groups, and an objective one connected with the type and complexity of the medical act. The system's flexibility is found in the movement of chronological limits, since the law sets forth presumptions that can be questioned such as maturity or immaturity in each concrete case, and the characteristics of the act as invasive or non-invasive, risky for the health condition. Both issues are to be solved by the judge.'[60]

186. As it is mentioned in the Commented Civil and Commercial Code in charge of Dr Ricardo Lorenzetti – Supreme Court Justice Member – section 26 'there has been an evolution as from the strict provisions of the Code derogated regarding incompetency in fact, up to the current acceptance of a progressive competence adjusted to underage's age, sufficient level of maturity and their insertion in the society to exercise the acts permitted under the provisions in force.'[61] This evolution empowers the underaged even in terms of their own body, according to the current reality and the challenges faced by those not over 18 years of age yet.

§2. The Mental Patient

187. Law 26657 – which establishes the Right to the Mental Health Protection – derogates Law 22914 and sets forth a change in paradigm in terms of mental healthcare and 'full enjoyment of human rights by those with mental ailments in national territory; human rights recognized in international instruments, with constitutional hierarchy, notwithstanding the beneficial regulations that for the protections of these rights the provinces and Buenos Aires city may establish'.

188. For a start, this regulation reinforces the capacity is presumed, that the rule is the capacity and not the other way about. The core reference arises from the Civil and Commercial Code of the Nation, among other principles, from section 22 which states that 'all human beings enjoy the aptitude to be owners of legal rights and

60. 'El consentimiento informado de las personas menores de edad' Fama, María Victoria; article published in the DELS, available at https://salud.gob.ar/dels/entradas/el-consentimiento-informado-de-las-personas-menores-de-edad.
61. 'Commented Civil and Commercial Code of the Nation', in charge of Ricardo Luis Lorenzetti; Book I; page 115; Rubinzal Culzoni Publishers.

duties' and that at the same time, 'the law can deprive or limit that capacity regarding events, simples acts or certain legal acts, accordingly'.

189. The State recognizes in favour of those with a mental illness a series of rights provided in section 7 of Law 26657 which inevitably establishes the relationship between patients and relatives, healthcare professionals and medical institutions:

(a) The right to receive integral, medical, social, and humanized assistance with free, equal, and equitable access to the necessary services and supplies so as to ensure the recovery and preservation of the health.
(b) The right to know and preserve their identity, their group of belonging, genealogy, and history.
(c) The right to receive the assistance based on scientific underpinnings aligned with ethical principles.
(d) The right to receive treatment and to be treated with the most convenient therapeutic alternative which the least restrict their liberties and rights thus encouraging their communal, familiar, and labour integration.
(e) The right to be accompanied before, during and after the treatment by their relatives, other beloved ones, or those the person with a mental illness choose to that effect.
(f) The right to receive and reject spiritual or religious assistance.
(g) The right of the patient, his relative, or the person he appoints to have access to the family background, and medical records.
(h) The right to periodical supervision of the conditions by the competent authority in the case of involuntary or voluntary prolonged hospital admission.
(i) The right neither to be identified nor discriminated due to a current or past mental illness.
(j) the right to be suitably and comprehensively informed of the rights he is entitled to and to all the information regarding his health and treatment according to the regulations of informed consent, including all the alternatives for his assistance that in the case the patient is not able to understand shall be informed to his relatives, tutors, or legal representatives.
(k) The right to take decisions about his assistance and treatment within his capability.
(l) the right to receive a personalized assistance in a suitable environment with protection of his intimacy, always being recognized as a holder of rights, with full respect for his private life and freedom of communication.
(m) The right to not be a subject of clinical research or experimental treatments without his verifiable consent.
(n) The right for that mental illness not to be considered as something that cannot be modified
(o) The right not to be subject to forced jobs.
(p) The right to receive a fair compensation for his labour in case of participating in activities such as labour therapies or community service which might imply the production of objects, works, or services that can be commercialized afterwards.

190. Apart from National regulations, local ones are to be considered. For instance, Buenos Aires city has the Mental Health Act N° 448, from the year 2000 – which also recognizes concrete and specific rights in favour of all individuals in connection with the Mental Health System, namely:

191. The rights recognized by the National Constitution, the Convention of Children's Rights and other international treaties, the Buenos Aires City Constitution, and the Law n°153 under its sections 4°:

- The right to the identity, genealogy, and history.
- The right to respect, dignity, singularity, autonomy, and consideration of family and social bonds of patients undergoing treatment.
- The right not to discriminated for suffering or having suffered a mental illness.
- The right to suitable and comprehensive information inherent to health and treatment including alternatives for assistance.
- The right to make decisions in relation to their assistance and treatment.
- The right to assistance based on scientific groundwork adjusted to social and ethical principles.
- The right to a personalized treatment and integral assistance in an environment suitable for the protection of their intimacy.
- The right to the use of the most convenient therapeutic alternative the least limiting in terms of their freedom.
- The right to rehabilitation and family and labour reinsertion into the community.
- The right to have contact with their relatives and others in the accompaniment of the children and teenagers admitted in hospital, unless otherwise indicated by the professional.

§3. The Dying Patient

192. Law 26742 – also known as the 'Dignified Death Act'-, of the year 2012, introduced important modifications to the regulation which established the patient's rights in their relationship with healthcare professionals and institutions (26529). So, the first issue to be analysed in relation to the terminally ill patient, consecrates the autonomy of will, a right provided in section 1 of the law, subsection e.

193. The referred subsection clearly specifies that 'the patient is entitled to accept or reject certain biological or medical procedures or therapies, with or without expressing the cause, as well as to further revoke his manifestation of will. Children and teenagers have to right to intervene in the terms of the Law 26061 concerning the decision-making of biological or medical procedures or therapies in which their health or life could be involved.'

194. In the frame of this power, the patient presenting an irreversible, incurable illness, or being in a terminal condition, or having suffered injuries placing him in such condition, clearly informed, has the right to manifest his will concerning the rejection of surgical procedures, or those of artificial reanimation or the withdrawal of the life-sustaining measure when they are extraordinary or disproportionate in relation to the perspective of improvement, or when experiencing excruciating pain. He shall as well be entitled to reject hydration or feeding procedures when they produce a unique effect that of prolonging terminal, irreversible and incurable condition in time. (Such are the words of paragraph 2º if this subsection e).

195. This section further states that in all cases the rejection or refusal of the mentioned procedures shall not mean the interruption of such measures or actions for the proper control and relief of the patient´s suffering. Here it is vital to make a clear difference among between 'dignified death', euthanasia, assisted suicide and pious killing. It is worth noticing the categorization made by Luis Guillermo Blanco:[62] while rejecting a therapy or treatment implies the patient's non-transferrable right, the euthanasia could be defined as the medical act by means of which – at the patient's request – a patient's life is deliberately, prematurely, and directly ended (caused death) so as to finish with the agony. Euthanasia is not regulated in Argentina yet.

196. In the case of assisted suicide – which implies murder – the interested party resorts to lethal means to end his own life, lethal means provided by a third party (whose collaboration entails a reproachable behaviour legally speaking). In pious murder, also typified as a crime in Argentina (not autonomous, without distinction with murders) a person kills another to release the latter from psychosomatic unbearable suffering.[63]

197. The provisions under section 2 subsection e reinforces that 'the patient shall exercise the right set forth under section 2, subsection e), paragraph 3 of the Law N°26529, amended by Law Nº 26742, when he suffers from an irreversible, incurable illness and is in a terminal condition, or has suffered injuries placing him in such condition. In the case of discrepancies in the decisions, a bioethics committee could intervene.'

198. In conjunction with what has so far been elaborated, section 11 of the Law of the Patient's Rights refers to the expression known as 'anticipated directives' which 'constitute a voluntary document containing instructions drafted by a person in full possession of his mental faculties, to be used when he is not able to express his will', the way Eleonora Lamm, bioethics, and law PHD, puts it.[64] It is a declaration of will done by a person so that his will is respected in case he is bereft of his capacity due to a supervening cause: a kind of anticipated informed consent.

---

62. 'Morir con dignidad'; Blanco, Luis Guillermo; article published in the DELS available at https://salud.gob.ar/dels/entradas/morir-con-dignidad#:~:text=Morir%20con%20dignidad%20(o%20morir, que%20un%20paciente%20puede%20l%C3%ADcitamente.
63. Also defined by Dr Blanco, existing in section 'Homicidio piadoso', published by DELS and available at https://salud.gob.ar/dels/entradas/homicidio-piadoso.
64. 'Directivas médicas anticipadas'; Lamm, Eleonora; article published by DELS, available at https://salud.gob.ar/dels/entradas/directivas-medicas-anticipadas#:~:text=Las%20directivas%20anticipadas.,no%20pueda%20expresar%20su%20voluntad.

199. After all these regulations, the Civil and Commercial Code of the Nation also incorporated the anticipated directives. Section 60 establishes that 'a person with full capacity can anticipate directives and confer powers regarding his health in prevision of his own incapacity', being able at the same time to appoint a person or persons that will express such consent for the execution of the medical acts and for his guardianship. Nevertheless, the directives implying the development of euthanasic practices are conceived as non-written, thus the long-standing debate in that respect and the way to instrument it. Numerous bills were introduced in the National Congress but with no concrete result.

200. Last but not least, section 61 of the CCCN refers to the remains of the person after he dies, his destinations, and the person's right with capacity to dispose of, by any means, the way and circumstances of his funeral rites and inhumation, as well as to give all or part of his body for therapeutical, scientific, pedagogical means or otherwise. 'In the case the deceased's will has not been expressed' – under the referred section – 'or it is not presumed, the decision shall be in the hands of the spouse, co-habitant or the relatives in the succession order, who cannot give to the dead body a destination different from that of the deceased if he had been able to express his will.'

Chapter 3. Specific Activities

§1. Abortion

201. Argentina has had a law stipulating the Voluntary Interruption of Pregnancy (IVE by its acronym in Spanish) since January 2021, the date on which Law 27610 became effective. Due to the obvious ethical, religious, and political commitment, the introduction of this legislation was not harmonious: even though a similar project was debated in the National Congress in the year 2018 – with the approval of representatives but not of the senate – the debate of the legislators' unleashed euphoria and expectation even outside the rooms, among those in favour and against the Voluntary Interruption of the Pregnancy.

202. Apart from addressing the voluntary interruption of pregnancy, law 27610 establishes post-abortion assistance, 'in compliance with the commitments undertaken by the Argentinean State concerning the public health and the human rights of the women and other persons with the ability to give birth and so as to contribute to reduce the foreseeable mortality and morbidity', as the rule reads. The law gives the pregnant person the right to decide, with no further third party's intervention, not even the progenitor or a person with the capacity to give birth.

203. Hence, section 2 of the IVE Act establishes for women and individuals with the ability to give birth, the right:

(a) To decide the voluntary early interruption of the pregnancy pursuant to regulations set forth in the current law.
(b) To require and access to assistance in the voluntary early interruption of a pregnancy in the health system services pursuant to regulations set forth in the current law.
(c) To require and receive post abortion assistance in health system services, without detriment of the decision of early interruption of pregnancy would have been contrary to the cases legally authorized.
(d) To prevent the non-intentional pregnancies by means of access to information, integral sexual education and to efficient contraceptive methods.

204. The decision of the individuals empowered to decide and access to the IVE must be taken until week fourteen of the pregnancy, unless: (1) the pregnancy was the result of rape, with the pregnant person's corresponding request and affidavit before the intervening healthcare personnel; or (2) in case the pregnant person's life or integral health was in danger. In these two cases, the assistance shall be provided even after the week fourteen of the pregnancy.

205. The access to IVE must be done within ten days of its request, the healthcare personnel must give humane treatment to the requesting individual, behave with respect towards the patient's privacy – information is given to the family only in the case the pregnant person expressly authorizes it – keep the due confidentiality during the treatment and after the abortion procedure, respect the requesting party's free will and decisions, keep an active and respectful listening and cover certain quality standards during the process.

206. One of the most controversial issues of the regulation is when it refers to the physician's moral objection. Although law 27610 recognizes this right of the healthcare professionals, it also sets forth certain guidelines regarding its exercise: the decision must be coherent in all the fields where he/she practices the profession; the patient must be derived to be assisted without delay; and he must perform all his duties as a physician. Moral objection shall not proceed when the pregnant person's life or integral health is at risk, and she needs immediate assistance. Neither shall it be valid in the case of post-abortion assistance.

207. The same regulation establishes guidelines for healthcare institutions when expressing that 'those healthcare institutions of the private subsector or of the social security not having professionals to perform the interruption of the pregnancy due to moral objection pursuant to the section, shall be liable to provide and dispose of the patient referral to a similar healthcare institution that can effectively provide the service. In all cases, the performance of this operation must be guaranteed under the dispositions of the present law. Formalities as well as costs associated to the referral and transfer of the patient will be performed by the healthcare institution in charge of the referral. All referrals contemplated in this section shall be billed based on the coverage and in favour of the healthcare institution that will effectively perform the procedure' (section 11).

208. Section 11 introduces a fundamental guideline of this law: the users' unrestrictive access, without dependence on costs that will be expected by the union-run insurance companies, pre-paid medicine companies and even by the State. The inclusion of the IVE in the Medical Obligatory Plan (PMO) completes the free integral coverage of the practice, a fundamental way to deal with one of the reasons shaping the sanction of this law: the clandestine abortions in places of dubious origin without control in which women without financial resources are treated to support consulting rooms that even acting beyond the law, try to keep the hygiene and minimum care conditions, in Argentina.

209. The design of the new legal framework concerning health brought about changes in criminal regulations: among other issues, it is established that 'the abortion performed with the pregnant person's consent until fourteen (14) weeks (inclusive) of pregnancy is not typified as a crime'. Thus, apart from the introductions concerning health, the elimination of punitive acts for crimes typified by law or punished by the legislation accompanies the IVE, this new legal classification.

§2. STERILISATION

210. 'Regime for the contraception surgical methods' is the title of Law 26130 which establishes the limits and scope of the right every overaged person is entitled to, in order to access tubal ligation and vasectomy in healthcare services. To make use of the power, the user must formally request it with the corresponding informed consent.

211. The same as in the case of Voluntary Interruption of Pregnancy, these contraceptive procedures must be performed at no cost for the patients; those responsible for these interventions should be union-run insurance companies, pre-paid medicine companies and the State (these types of procedures must be 'free of charge' for the beneficiaries according to the regulation).

212. The moral objection in these cases may be issued by the professional without any labour-related consequence for him; however, this objection does not exempt the healthcare institution authorities from responsibility regarding the realization of the required practice. Hence, the healthcare institution must dispose of necessary replacements without further delay.

§3. In Vitro Fertilization (Law 26862: On Integral Access to Medical-Assisted Techniques and Procedures of Medically Assisted Reproduction)

213. A plexus of Regulations avant-garde, under its section 8, sets forth the core of the law: 'The public health sector, the union-run health insurance plans framed in laws 23660 and 23661, health insurance of the National Judicial Power, Social Assistance Bureau for the National Congress' Staff, pre-paid medicine entities and entities providing services to university staff, as well as all providers rendering medically assisted services to their members regardless of their legal frame, shall guarantee to their members – as obligatory benefits – integral interdisciplinary coverage namely: diagnosis, medicine and supporting therapies, and procedures, techniques that the World Health Organization defines as medically assisted reproduction, such as: ovulation induction; controlled ovarian hyperstimulation; ovulation triggers; assisted reproduction techniques (TRA); and intrauterine, intracervical, intravaginal or intrauterine insemination, with the partner's gametes or not, or with those of a donor according to the criteria established by the authority of application.'

214. It even goes further: 'all these procedures are included in the (PMO), as well as those of diagnosis, medicinal and support therapies, and the criteria and modalities of coverage established by the authority of application, which will not be able to include requirements or limitations – implying the exclusion – due to sexual orientation or the marital status of the beneficiaries. Also contained in the coverage under this section, are the custody services of gametes or reproductive cells, with the best technology available and authorized to that end by the authority of application for those people, even people under eighteen (18) years of age who do not wish to get immediately pregnant and due to health problems or medical treatment or surgical intervention may have a disability to reproduce in the future.'

215. The regulation seems to be transparent and clear; however, it has triggered a lot of debate regarding its observance[65] and has given place to a complementary regulation limiting access to certain practices or treatments. This is the case of the Resolution I-E/2017 of the Health Ministry, which set forth the scopes and implications of a medically assisted reproduction treatment with high-complexity medical TRA (TRHA/AC) which each patient is entitled to; or the case of Resolution 1044/2018, which established that all reproductive treatment medically assisted with her own ovules will be performed on women up to 44 years of age at the moment of accessing such treatment, unless medically prescribed otherwise; and to women up to 51 years of age in case of donated ovules.

216. Other controversies about this regulation had to be solved by justice. One of the main debates is about how many high-complexity treatments one person with health insurance is entitled to perform. The regulation of Law 26862 establishes that 'a person shall be entitled to have access to a maximum of FOUR (4) treatments a year with low-complexity medically assisted reproduction techniques, and up to THREE (3) treatments with high-complexity medically assisted techniques with minimum intervals of Three (3) months in between them'. Not being explicit if the treatments of high complexity were up to three per year or in total; a criterium supported the interpretation of the annual period; and another interpretation – popular among those having to cover the treatment – which claimed that the person was entitled to three treatments in total throughout life.

217. The Supreme Court of the Nation established the annual obligation in a concrete precedent: 'from the text of the law 26862 it arises that said law guarantees the integral access to the medically – assisted techniques and procedures of medically-assisted reproduction leading to conclude that the law-maker has intended to ensure that coverage shall guarantee the full exercise of the right to reproductive health within a wide scope since it is closely related to the fundamental right to life. The only limit that the law sets in that respect is in connection to those techniques and procedures not specified in the very same rule, or to those not approved by the authority of application (last paragraph, section 2, Law 26862). In this sense, the Decree 956/2013 when providing the maximum of three high-complexity treatments does not clearly say if it is three in total or three in a specific period. However, a complete reading of the rule helps understand that the limit of three interventions has been established in relation to the annual period that was explicitly set forth for the coverage of low complexity techniques mentioned in the first paragraph (in this case four). The rule has been drafted in only one paragraph or sentence and so the absence of the time reference in the case of high complexity

65. Law 26862 is understood to regulate in matters implying personal, ethical, and religious convictions which are not only related to the notion of family but also the process used to get there. In such delicate talks, personal interests and perceptions are introduced which often hinder the observance of the law.

techniques of assisted reproduction is just for the sake of economy of speech to avoid the unnecessary repetition of the word "annual".'[66]

218. Even though the basis for coverage established by law is wide, the Supreme Court has also set a limit for certain treatments, such as for example the Preimplantation Genetic Diagnosis, (PGD).[67]

§4. Prenatal Diagnosis (Genetics in General)

219. The regulations preventing and protecting prenatal health have been formulated together with technological breakthroughs and the awareness of early healthcare. Hence, in the year 2003, the National Health Ministry passed the Resolution 648/2003 approving the document 'The Pre-Natal Care Guide for the Practice of Pre-conceptional Care and Prenatal Control', forming part of the National Program of Quality Guarantees in the Medical Attention. The document – focused on the healthcare Teams and aimed at providing procedures, practices and technologies of approved clinical efficiency, contributes to improving the quality of the work realized in the perinatal field and serves as the basis for the revision of regulations which apply to health services.

220. The Medical Obligatory Plan (PMO), whose main preventive more than healing objective guides the way for the Argentinean Health Law, devotes several parts to the approach of the Maternal Infantile Plan (PMI by its acronym in Spanish). Thus, this basic coverage program includes everything concerning pregnancy and delivery from the moment of diagnosis to the first month after birth.

221. The newly born baby assistance until one year of age must be 100% coverage for inpatients as well as for outpatients, except for payment of any type of co-insurance for specific medicines and assistance. This coverage is for consultations, and diagnosis studies exclusively related to pregnancy, delivery, and post-pregnancy since other types of studies will be covered by the PMO; obstetric psychoprophylaxis, medicines exclusively related to pregnancy and delivery with 100% coverage. In turn, as regards children's health, it is obligatory to perform a perinatological study for the detection of phenylketonuria, congenic hypothyroidism, and fibrocystic illness in the newly born. Follow-up and control consultations, immunizations of the period should be covered; 100% coverage of any required medication throughout the first year of age will be covered as long as it is on the list of indispensable medicines.

222. In the year 2021, Law 27611 – of Integral Healthcare and Assistance during the pregnancy and first infancy – repeats this idea of the cited legislation so as

66. Decision 'Y., M. V. and others against Instituto de Obra Social del Ejército (IOSE) about Amparo on health'; CSJN; 14/08/2018; Rubinzal Online; 4612/2014; RC J 5184/18.
67. National Supreme Court Decision in case entitled 'De-facto appeal filed by the plaintiff in the case entitled L.E.H. and others against O.S.E.P. about amparo'.

to strengthen the integral care of women and other pregnant persons' health and life and that of children in first infancy. Section 21 established the 'specific strategies for perinatal and first years' health'; and the application authority is responsible for the implementation of the specific assistance, promotion, protection, and prevention health policies for integral health of pregnant persons and children up to (3) three years of age. Among other aspects, women and other pregnant persons' access to health assistance to perform controls and duly interventions and in an integral way to prevent, diagnose and treat eventual complications is fostered in the healthcare system.

§5. Organ Transplants (Law 27447: On Tissue, Organs, and Cells Transplants)

223. It regulates 'activities related to the acquirement and use of organs, tissue and cells of human origin, in the whole territory of Argentina, including the research, promotion, donation, extraction, preparation, distribution, the transplant and further follow-up'. It also contains donors' and receptors' rights, issues related to professionals, services and to institutions, as well as punishment and fines for those not respecting the prohibitions therein contained. This law also regulates all matters related to the National Central Institute – Unique Ablation and Implant Coordinator (INCUCAI by its acronym in Spanish), public entity of public law which is in the frame of the Health Ministry and that oversees the quality, the security, and the traceability of donation processes and organs, tissues and cells transplant of in Argentina, amongst other areas.

224. Even though it is a very complex set of rules amended in the last years – the text in force today is from the year 2018-. Regarding section 28 of this instrument, it is noteworthy, that 'in no case whatsoever shall the expenses connected with the ablation and/or implant and the medical treatment, be at the expense of the donor or their beneficiaries. Said expenses must be covered by the entity in charge of the social or sanitary coverage of the receiver, or the receiver itself when he does not have a social security.'[68] This section summarizes the pillars of the system: equity and solidarity. Likewise, this section must guarantee the patients free selection of the authorized transplant centre. This should be pointed out since the user cannot freely choose the provider; in general, the beneficiary only has the options in a list of professionals provided by his union-run health insurance plan or by the prepaid medicine company (in the case of the public coverage, this is even more restricted). The legislation constitutes an exception on this point.

68. Law 24193 – of 1995, prior to law 27447 and derogated by the latter, already contemplated this atypical power of the user, which clearly depicts the tradition and maturity of the system and the essence we have been elaborating so far.

225. 'The Public Health System is liable to cover all the expenses of those patients who do not have a Health Insurance – public or private- and whose financial situation does not allow them to afford it', section 28 of this law is, once again, in harmony with the general spirit of the Argentinean Health Law.

§6. Experiments on Human Beings

226. Disaggregated is the local legislation regulating experimentation on human subjects. The Civil and Commercial Code of the Nation, due to the lack of a concrete law – and setting aside the ethical guidelines on the subject – shed light on this aspect, elaborated in section 58 of the cited legislation.

227. Said section 58 set forth requirements for medical research in human beings by means of interventions such as treatments, prevention methods, diagnostic or predictive tests whose efficiency and safety are not scientifically proved. The requirements are namely:

(a) to clearly describe the project and method to be applied in the research protocol;
(b) to be performed by people with the suitable professional and scientific expertise and qualifications to that end;
(c) to have the prior consent by an authorized Ethical Evaluation Committee in research;
(d) to have the prior authorization of the corresponding public agency;
(e) to be based upon the careful comparison of risks and loads in relation to the foreseeable benefits represented for the people participating in the research and for other people affected by the topic being researched;
(f) to have the prior written free informed and specific consent of the persons participating in the research who shall be fully advised about the objectives, research methodology, the risk and possible benefits in comprehensible terms; such consent shall be revocable;
(g) not to imply for the participant risks and pains disproportionate in relation to the benefits expected to be obtained by means of the research;
(h) to protect the participant's intimacy and their personal information confidentiality during the research;
(i) the ensure that the participants' collaboration in the research is not onerous for them and they shall have access to suitable and timely medical assistance in the case of adverse events related to the research;
(j) to ensure the participant availability and accessibility to the treatment that the research has proved to be beneficial.

§7. Euthanasia

228. Argentina has no legislation regulating euthanasia. There are some projects that have gained notoriety in the media but are still sitting in Congress without approval. All this regardless of the differences among 'dignified death', assisted suicide and pious murder, distinctions already elaborated in Chapter 2, §3 (The dying patient).

§8. OTHERS (TRANSSEXUAL INTERVENTIONS)

229. In 2012, the Gender Identity Law (26743) gave rise to rights in favour of liberty and diversity. With a wording which is a novelty for other compared legislation, it recognized the Gender Identity for all persons, everyone's free development according to such identity and the right to be treated accordingly, and specially, to be identified in that way in the documents accrediting their identity concerning their first name, photograph and gender therein registered.

230. In that respect, section 11 of that regulation establishes that 'all person older that eighteen (18) years of age shall be entitled to, pursuant to Section 1 of said law, and to guarantee the enjoyment of their integral health, to have access to total or partial surgical operations and/or hormone integral treatments to adjust their body, their genitals included, to their self-perceived gender identity, without the necessary judicial or administrative authorization.'

231. The very same section provides that 'to have access to the integral hormone treatments, it will not be necessary to express the will in the surgical intervention of the total or partial genital reassignment. In both cases, it will only be necessary the person's informed consent.' In the case of the underaged, the legal representative shall intervene with the minor's expressed consent. 'Notwithstanding that' – the section further establishes – in the case of the informed consent procurement 'regarding the total or partial surgery, it shall further be necessary to have each jurisdiction competent judicial authority's conformity, who shall have to ensure the child's principles of progressive capacity and superior interest pursuant to what is set forth under the Convention on Children's Rights and under Law 26061 of the Children's and Teenagers' Rights Integral Protection. The judicial authority shall inform in a term not longer than (60) sixty days as from the date of the request.'

232. The coverage of the surgical interventions and treatments herein mentioned are incorporated into the Medical Obligatory Plan (PMO), thus the costs are assumed by the healthcare providers – public, private or those of the union-run insurance companies – who have the obligation to guarantee those rights permanently.

233. Law 26743 laid new foundations for the expansion of the rights concerning identity and self-perception. It is a very complex issue, yet to be fully developed, which is advancing together with the cultural changes and new paradigms imposing amendments in the local legislation. One of the latest changes is reflected in the Resolution 3159/2019 of the Ministry of Health and Social Development which added cyproterone Acetate, gel Testosterone, gel 17ß-oestradiol, oestradiol Valerate, Spironolactone, Testosterone and Triptorelin Undecanoate to the PMO with

100% coverage for patients under an integral hormone treatment to change secondary features corresponding to the gonadal sex for the adjustment of the image to the self-perceived gender.

Part III. The Physician in Relation to the Healthcare System

Chapter 1. Collegial Relationships

§1. ASSOCIATIONS

234. On the roles and the relationship between physicians and professional associations, there is a reference under the title 'Freedom of establishment' in Part I, Chapter I. At the same time, it was further mentioned the Argentinean Medical Association (AMA) – one of the oldest and most important institutions in the country – under the title 'Order of physicians'. On the other hand, it is worth noticing that relationship among the different medical institutions is not regulated, and it is – in general terms – contingent and circumstantial. The aim of individual work generally coincides with that of the group: they are the sounding boards of professionals' needs and worries resulting from their job and the errors and corrections yet to be made in the healthcare system.

235. The pandemic caused by COVID-19 foregrounded the importance of these professional associations and their relationship with one another. One of the main collective efforts was in October which implied the drafting of the document in which 28 medical associations from Argentina agreed on the risk in the interruption of consultations, of diagnosis tests and of certain interventions.[69]

§2. HEALTHCARE CENTRES

236. Law 17132 – on the Art of Healing – stipulates under its section 34 that 'any person intending to have an institution for the prophylaxis, recovery, diagnosis and/or treatment of human diseases, must require the corresponding permit from the Public Health State Secretary, containing a statement related to the orientation of the activities of such institution, with the specific kind and modality of services to cover and the modalities of payment on behalf of the beneficiaries.' So as to get authorization, 'the interested party must show that the facilities meet all requirements

69. For further information the website of the Cámara Argentina de Especialidades Medicinales (CAEME) https://www.caeme.org.ar/28-sociedades-medicas-de-argentina-se-unen/.

under the law herein, in relation to equipment, medical instruments, number of professionals, specialists, and assistants, considering the aim of their activity, of the services rendered, as well as that due to the location it does not entail a risk for public health.'

237. These establishments must meet the criteria established in the corresponding regulations, adapted to the objectives, specialties, facilities, equipment, medical instruments, number of professionals and paramedics for the provision of these services. After obtaining the authorization, they will not be able to change the company name or company name, nor will they be able to reduce their services without authorization. The violation of these rules will lead to the preventive closure of the establishments.

Chapter 2. Relationship with Other Healthcare Providers

§1. Pharmacists

238. Law 17565 establishes the Legal Regime of the Pharmaceutical Activity, and the Pharmacies, Drugstores and Herbalists' shop authorization. Such regulation from the year 1967 had significant amendments in 2009, by means of Law 26567.

239. Among other related issues, this Regime establishes that preparation of prescriptions, sale of drugs, medicines, even those so-called over the counter and those of pharmaceutical specialty, no matter how they are sold, will only be done on the national territory, in pharmacies only licensed by the competent sanitary authority who in turn has the power of control and supervision.

240. This legislation establishes that over-the-counter medicines must be sold by pharmacists themselves or those authorized to that effect. In case the medicines were sold outside the premises of the pharmacy that would be considered illegal trade and, notwithstanding sanctions established under law, those responsible could be accused of a criminal offense.

241. Pursuant to the legislation in force, there exist four modalities of selling drugs, or medicines: legally restricted ones, with a filed prescription, with a prescription and over the counter. The prescriptions corresponding to the first two categories must be kept in paper or digital format for at least three years. At the end of this period, they can be destroyed or deleted by notifying the health authorities in advance.

242. The pharmacy must be managed by a technical director who is responsible to the authorities for compliance with all rules, laws, regulations and duties applicable in the jurisdiction in which the establishments under his supervision are located. The responsibility of the technical director does not exclude the responsibility of other professionals or collaborators, nor the legal or physical owners of the facilities. Any change in the technical management of the pharmacy, whether temporary or permanent, must be approved by the health authority. The technical director must be a pharmacist with a doctorate in pharmacy or in pharmacy and biochemistry. Under no circumstances may a professional pharmacist be technical manager in more than one pharmacy. He is required to personally and efficiently maintain the premises, to supervise the preparation and sale of medicines and to sign the prescription pad daily under the last prescription sent.

243. The pharmacist is responsible for the purity and origin of the products he sends or uses in his preparations, as well as the substitution of products, changes in dosage and the incorrect preparation of medicines. In the case of special medicines, he is only responsible for their legitimacy, origin and conservation. The technical manager must proceed with the preparation and sale of drugs in accordance with the prescriptions established by the doctor and with all the provisions of the National Pharmacopoeia, unless otherwise specified by the doctor. If he believes that the prescription contains an error, he will not send it and at the same time will ask the doctor to clarify the case accordingly.

244. This law further enumerates a series of specific prohibitions for pharmacists, namely:

(a) To announce, have in stock and sell medicines of secret or mysterious composition.
(b) To announce and sell therapeutic agents with infallible or extraordinary effects or offering radical cure to any disease.
(c) To apply in their private practice procedures that were not presented or considered or approved in university or scientific centres in the country.
(d) To advertise by any means medications or specialties not recognized by sanitary authorities.
(e) To place by any means advertisements highlighting or faking virtues of therapeutic diagnostic, prophylactic or diet medicines, products, or agents.
(f) To publish personal procedures or techniques in non-specialized media.
(g) To exercise the profession while suffering from infectious-contagious diseases.
(h) To persuade their clients to buy certain medicines.
(i) To share fees with physicians and dentists.
(j) To obtain fees from clinical laboratories.
(k) To give powers, or attributions or to delegate roles inherent or exclusive of their profession to their assistant personnel.

§2. Nurses (Midwives)

245. Law 17132, passed in the year 1967 by decision of the de facto government is still in force and established under its section 49 that 'the practice of obstetrics is reserved to persons of the female gender in possession of the university degree of midwife'. Even though there is no legal amendment of the law – and there neither seems to be justification nowadays to make a difference between men and women – the local legislation ruling obstetrics practices in general has overcome this distinction of gender something that nowadays is seen as an act of discrimination.

246. This regulation further sets forth that 'Midwives will not be able to give assistance to pregnant women or those in labour or in pathological puerperium, and they will have to limit their job to their specific specialization; and in the case of any abnormal symptom in the course of the pregnancy, delivery and/or puerperium, they are obliged to request a physician's presence, specialized in obstetrics if possible.' In turn, assistance in official or private healthcare institutions (approved to that effect), in the patient's domicile or in the physician's consulting room is also authorized.

247. To admit pregnant persons in their consulting room, the midwives must have prior authorization from the corresponding authority. The denomination

'Maternities or Maternal Clinics' will be reserved for the installations having medical management and a body of physicians specialized in obstetrics.

248. Even though law 17132 – as a legal framework – still regulates the practice of obstetrics at a national level, it is a very old law and out of date in terms of current needs of patients and the professionals acting in obstetrics. Thus, it is necessary to pay attention to each local (provincial) legislation to have a more comprehensive view of this branch of medicine. The lack of regulation according to the present time and the spirit of Argentine health law has led to several complaints from obstetric organizations and even from the Argentine Obstetrics Association (FORA with its Spanish acronym) asking for an amendment and an update of Law 17132 by the National Congress[70] to fill the gaps of this no longer relevant legislation.

§3. Paramedical Professionals

249. At a national level, Argentina does not have legislation to define and clearly regulate the activity of paramedics, emergency room services, or professionals connected with the prehospital practice. Nevertheless, there are grounds in the National Congress to create the legislation accordingly.

250. Certain local legislation seems to be innovative in the matter. Buenos Aires city, for example, as from law 1883 regulated the System of Medical Assistance in the Emergency Room (SAME by its acronym in Spanish) aiming at 'rendering of the healthcare service in situations of emergency and/or extra hospital or prehospital emergency understood as a coordination operational service for urgent medical problems in all medical assistance and transport services rendered to ill people outside the hospital as a previous instance to hospital urgency or treatment'. In Buenos Aires city, there also exists Law 5469 of Ambulance Terrestrial System which defines extra hospital medical emergency and establishes guidelines concerning the non-state ambulance systems.

251. In a different vein, law 15094 of Buenos Aires province provides the legal regime on professional practice of medical emergency technicians. Other provinces also have local legislation mainly focused on providing guidelines due to absence of an integral and precise regulation on the matter.

70. The demand made by the Obstetrics personnel is registered and updated in the official website of FORA, of public access at http://fora-obstetricas.org/index.php/ley-de-obstetricas.

Chapter 3. Relationship with Healthcare Institutions

§1. Hospitals

252. By means of Decree 939/2000, the National Executive Power, the Decentralized – Management Public Hospital Regime was created (HPGD), with the aim to implement instrumental and Substantive Policies fixed to the National Administration for transformation, development and strengthening of health sector, and to correct certain issues on behalf of the Self-management Public Hospital Regime.

253. Thus, this new regime was conceived with five objectives:

(a) To foster actions tending to increment hospital budgets by means of an income obtained for the collection of services rendered to beneficiaries by other health sub-systems.
(b) To promote the rational and efficient management of health.
(c) To improve levels of accessibility for the population without insurance.
(d) To respect regional and local specification of institutions with support and consolidation of a federal conception of health.
(e) To increase the commitment of personnel with institutions as from the distribution of a percentage of the income obtained through the collection of the billing presented.

254. This legal framework gave decentralized-management public hospitals several powers, such as to enter into agreements – by means of the competent jurisdictional authority – with entities such as union-run insurance companies; to collect money from eventual services rendered by the union-run insurance companies, insurance mutuals, and pre-paid medicine companies; and to dispose of the earning generated by the hospital itself, among other things.

255. Among the duties of the hospitals, there are: to comply with the basic requirements established by National Program to Guarantee Quality in Medical Assistance, to have authorization and categorization of a competent enterprise; to exercise management of personnel, to have their own internal regulations and to constitute technical counselling commissions and/or committees

Selected Bibliography

*El libro de los presidentes argentinos del siglo XX (The book of the Argentinean Presidents of the twentieth Century) 2000, Ed. Aguilar, Buenos Aires, Argentina.

'La responsabilidad del médico de guardia en el Código Civil y Comercial'; Noriega, Nina Norma; Ed. Rubinzal Culzoni, 'RC D 1120/2017'.

'La responsabilidad civil de los médicos luego de la sanción del nuevo Código Civil y Comercial', Musacchio, Carolina Inés; Ed. Rubinzal Culzoni, 'RC D 1849/ 2016'.

'Responsabilidad del médico generalista', Vázquez Ferreyra, Roberto A.; Revista de Derecho de Daños, año 2003, Tomo III, Responsabilidad de los profesionales de la salud, Ed. Rubinzal Culzoni, 'RC D 1204/2012'.

'Commented Civil and Commercial Code of the Nation', in charge of Ricardo Luis Lorenzetti; Book I; page 115; Rubinzal Culzoni Publishers.

'El juicio de amparo'; Gozaìni, Osvaldo Alfredo; Rubinzal Culzoni Editores.

Selected Bibliography

Index

The numbers here refer to paragraph numbers

Index